My Secret Self:

SERIES - BOOK THREE

Death And The
Cycles of Life

Christine U. Cowin

My Secret Self: Death And The Cycles of Life
First published in Australia by Christine U. Cowin 2020
www.christineucowinwriter.com
www.amazon.com/author/christineucowinwriter

Prepublication Data Service details available from
The National Library of Australia
ISBN: 978-0-6484013-4-6 (pbk)
ISBN: 978-0-6484013-5-3 (ebk)

Typesetting and design by Publicious Book Publishing
Published in collaboration with Publicious Book Publishing
www.publicious.com.au

Dedication

I dedicate my book to all those who have crossed my path, offering me a chance to learn what I needed to learn. This story is my truth and there is no intention on my part to ever hurt or harm anybody, I just want to tell my true story. Thank you to all who have been a part of my life. Our journey together has enabled me to understand life and grow as a person. And for that I love you and appreciate you.

Other Books by Christine U. Cowin

My Secret Self. Book 1 - Trials and Tribulations of an Innocent, published in, September 2018

My Secret Self. Book 2 - Questioning Life in Marriage, published in, July 2019

My website contains my Bio, links to
purchase my books and reviews:
Website: www.christineucowinwriter.com
Email address: christine@christineucowinwriter.com
Amazon Central Authors Page:
www.amazon.com/author/christineucowinwriter

Life and its Misery

Life has given me a destiny to open a pathway,
A pathway to where?
To my inner hell and my outer shame, guilt and blame,
Where will it all lead?
As I plunge into this game of life,
Is it unfolding as it should?
Did I plan this or was it planned?
The game of life is like a puzzle and each piece will set
out a picture of a story.
What story am I creating to plaster on the walls of time?
Who will be in this story?
Characters evade me now,
But they will soon infiltrate the secret corners of my mind,
To release the secrets from their prison, to escape the
prison of time.
Mind, oh mind, you are the warden of time, and you
have no mercy on the soul of light,
You only think of your own demise and not the purity
of the soul.
Your ego is a mountain high; to place me in these games
I'm in,
How do I get away from you to be the light of my day?
You punish, torment and irritate the being that you
have encapsulated,
You show little mercy and patience as the being tries to
awaken to its full glory.

Oh, ego, you dwindling star,
Your days in this being's body are numbered,
As soon as I make the shifts, you're out on your tush
and I am free of your idiosyncrasies.
I bid you farewell and send you to hell,
You've tormented me enough – begone and stay away
and never return.
Your welcome is overdue and your use-by date is
deleted, and now I will defeat you.

By Christine U. Cowin

Introduction

My first book, *My Secret Self: Trials and Tribulations of an Innocent,* tells the story of my childhood through to my teens. On this journey I realised I was in a family that was dysfunctional and didn't understand me. In later years this dysfunction would cause me to be isolated in that family. I couldn't understand why I was blamed just on my own.

These people were sad and trapped in their own grief and unhappiness. In these emotional trials they faced, they forgot to care for my well-being. I was a different child and I knew things they never knew, and I was not scared, but they were. I grew up in their sadness, loneliness, regret, and resentment, but I forever remained happy. I left high school and got my freedom with a car and a job.

In my second book, *My Secret Self: Questioning Life in Marriage,* I'd just got my freedom. I was in a job and having fun. One of my work colleagues wanted me to go on a date with his brother. To appease him, I did. What a lovely man, who would have given me an easy life.

But fate had other ideas; there was another direction I had to take.

I took the calling that was presented to me. I was now in a marriage where this man had no idea of who

I was. For that matter, he had no idea who he was, and cared little about such questions. He possessed me and kept me close in his eyeshot. He had no need to worry, because to me marriage was sacred. I began to question: why is his family so similar to my own? Our house had to be perfect. It looked perfect. But it wasn't. There were many flaws; however, no one knew about those flaws. They were all a secret.

The man I chose would take me on a path of questioning life, to seek answers and gain deeper knowledge. What was I doing? Why did I have to follow that path? A path all too familiar. That led me to question: who am I, why am I here, and what am I to do here? The questions were both spiritual and mundane. I was trying to understand life and why things were as they were, as well as why people acted as they did.

In my third book, *My Secret Self: Death and the Cycles of Life,* as time moves on and my children grow up, I have messages come to me to tell me that someone has died or will die. Death will present itself to me and take loved ones from us. There's a deeper reason why some go before us and there are lessons for us to learn. My new job will make me realise just how much we seem to be in a school of learning, and that school is called *Life.*

Meanwhile, there's a lot I need to understand about myself. I am gifted and know things; however, there's more. A deeper awakening is stirring in me. My dreams are so real and I'm being pulled into this next phase of my life. Here I am, asking myself different questions. Am I just existing? Have I been biding my time and receiving small bits of information to set me on my true path, until I can leave this man? Can I make my escape to freedom? Is all we do worked out for us? Or is it us making the changes? Are we helped in some way? I am starting to realise there's a reason for everything. I am a seeker of knowledge and I want to know.

I have been presented with some clues to start me on this journey that somehow I lost the script for, on entering this world. Can I find this script? How will I do that? There are more answers to my life – I'm only touching the surface. I know I can't do the work that is calling me if I stay in this marriage.

Chapter 1

Job Changes

Around 1981, Javier decided to leave Harper's Foundry; he was sick of shift work, and a job opportunity came up at Coal Dynamics, where my father worked. This was when a lot of changes occurred, because the job didn't pay well. This meant we needed extra money. Javier tried to work on weekends in the construction companies to supplement our income, but he wasn't coping, and this was causing him to suffer some health problems. Little did I know, the universe was opening my doors for me to expand through. If only I understood that back then; boy, oh boy, I would have flown into the spiritual and gained knowledge of life much quicker. Javier's eyes began to deteriorate to a point where if he didn't have a special operation available to him, he'd end up with minus-twenty vision and eventually blind, like his brother Bernat. Dr Omar knew all of the family members and their eye problems, so he recommended an operation to Javier called keratometry, to reduce his vision loss. It was a new technique. I felt Javier should take the chance and have it done. So he did, and he had his corneas sliced, thirty-two slices per eye. It was a success; his glasses were reduced from minus ten to minus five and three. However, there was a side effect – he developed some night blindness. He had to be very careful driving at night; this annoyed him, but I said to try to look at the positive side of the operation and be grateful for the reduction in his glasses. He was lucky then; his brothers, Bernat and Vince, couldn't be operated on; their eyes were past the cut-off point for the operation.

Later on, Javier developed stomach problems. He'd always had stomach problems, but this time it was serious. He'd been taking lozenges for stomach aches for many years. It was Easter time and we were visiting his mum. Suddenly, at her house, he got very sick and became very pale. His brother John was really worried, so he took Javier to the hospital. I stayed at the house because I didn't feel anything for Javier. I wasn't too worried, and Javier had a tendency to play sick; I knew his games, although his face was deathly white. On their return from hospital, John informed us, 'Javier had a bleeding ulcer.'

'How bad was it?' I asked.

'Very bad. He has to go and see Dr King, a stomach specialist, on Tuesday after the holidays,' John answered. I looked at Javier as he hung his head with his bottom lip pouting. I could see he was well into his self-pity. I hated it when he got into those moods. Even though I was concerned, I wasn't concerned, because there was so much going on between us and my feelings towards Javier– had closed down.

We went to see Dr King. After many tests and investigations, Javier was diagnosed with a duodenal ulcer. He had to go to Dawson Hill Hospital for an operation, but he refused, asking Dr King if he could be operated on in Hastings Crossing Hospital. The doctor agreed. I tried to tell Javier it would be better for him to go to the Dawson Hill Hospital and not to worry about us. But no, he had to be close to home and to us. I don't know why, because to me it wasn't an issue to drive to Dawson Hill. Also, if he was in Dawson Hill Hospital, his family could visit him through the day.

So he was operated on in Hastings Crossing Hospital, and placed into the intensive care ward. He stayed there for about ten days. He was in a very bad way, suffering immense pain, which showed me his vulnerable side. Javier had little tolerance to pain, and he was forever asking for painkillers, which he couldn't get. The Ward Sister would tell him he wasn't allowed any over his quota. But Javier never understood what people told him, and he tried to get me to get the nurses to give him extra tablets. Of course, they wouldn't. He then started to accuse them of cheating him of his medication by saying they were keeping it for themselves and selling it. I was stunned that Javier would think such things about the staff.

Although there were stories about the nursing staff stealing drugs, it was good while he was in the intensive care unit, because we couldn't go up to see him other than during visiting hours. When he was allowed into the main ward, we visited him more often. It was a difficult time for Javier, and he seemed to have slowed down a lot. He had to be careful with what he ate, and we had to deal with medications and diets – which we had never had to, to date. After many doctor visits and a full recuperation, life got back to normal and gradually Javier recovered, and he was soon back to his old self again.

Javier had to have regular check-ups; he chose to do this at Hastings Crossing Hospital rather than go all the way to Dawson Hill Hospital. Doing this, we came into contact with lots of new doctors, specialising at our local hospital. I noticed these doctors were of ethnic origin. I was being noticed by some of those doctors; I was aware of it but dismissed it. There was one doctor in particular, Dr Derek, and Javier told me he was from the Moor race from Northern Africa. Dr Derek was a strikingly handsome man and he had very black skin. I felt something from him, and I could tell that he really liked me. He made it obvious on his part. I could feel his eyes on me, and so could Javier, causing Javier to look at me during the consultation. But I played it down, not letting Javier know I noticed what was happening. This doctor was so blatant; he was almost mesmerised by me. He'd be talking to Javier and looking at me. I was so shy, and feared Javier's reaction if I looked at another man, so I always averted my eyes in such situations. I guess I tried to be blind to many things to save complications. But that was one thing Javier needn't have worried or feared from me, because in marriage I was so faithful; marriage to me was sacred.

Javier's father had explained the history of the Moor people to me: how they invaded Spain and held possession of the southern part of the country for seven hundred years. Javier also told me stories of that history; he wasn't sure if his family line had a link to this race or not, but his father was very dark-skinned. Javier wasn't – he was fairer like his mother. There were some health

4

issues in Javier's family; his mother and Bernat had diabetes, Pia had lupus, and four of the brothers had very poor eyesight. Mixed races didn't worry me; I loved having a variety of races within our genetics, and I was proud of my Chinese influence.

There were some surprising events coming up in the family. John had left his wife Lois. He'd never contacted his own children from his first marriage since his first wife left him. His children were older and wanted to meet their father and reconnect with him, especially his son Mitchell – but it was short-lived, because John had little tolerance for them. I got to meet Mitchell and Zara, but not the oldest daughter, Marisa. Apparently, she was still scarred by John leaving them; she didn't want to see him. I understood that, because John was so unpredictable, and he could be in your life one minute and disappear out of it just as fast. Mitchell was the one who most wanted a father-and-son relationship, but their association only lasted a few months, so he came in and left just as quickly. Maybe their mother warned them, and they saw the truth for themselves.

Bianca's marriage had folded up and she was having lots of health problems. She was now seeing Pia's boyfriend's brother, Conrad, and she was pregnant with his baby.

In 1981, Gema married her fiancé of six months, Basil. It was a wonderful wedding and I was so happy for her. At long last, she could break free from her family. Now she was married, it also gave me permission to confront Javier with all the secrets about his family he'd been withholding from me. When he enraged me, I'd let loose and tell him what I knew, never telling him who told me. Gema was safe because she wasn't home, and he couldn't pinpoint her as my source. He probably thought I'd just found out. I became angrier because I wasn't coping with his shit about my family. So one day I exploded, reminding him of the skeletons in his own family's closet. I screamed out, 'You bastard, Javier, I'm sick of you telling me how bad my family was. I want you to know I know about Bianca and that Leonard is Nick's son, and Bianca is up to her third child to three different fathers.'

'Shut up, you bitch,' he threatened, raising his hand.

I stood in defiance, saying, 'No, I won't, and Alexandre's gay and your family is just as bad as everyone else's, and no different to other people's families. But you want me to think my family is the only imperfect family and yours is perfect – well, they're not.'

He turned his head; he was defeated. I said, 'You can't see any wrong in your family –your sisters are living with guys unmarried, at least my sister and brother are married. My dad might be a liar, but he doesn't take money from us.'

He glared at me, asking, 'What do you mean by that?'

'Nothing.' I paused. 'Just that all of your family's working lives, they've had to handover their wages to your parents, and what do your parents have to show for that? Nothing, no savings and neither does anyone else in your family have any savings.'

I'd said enough and I didn't want to get Gema into trouble, because if I mentioned Gema having to give her father money to go out, he'd know who'd told me. But I was wound up and needed to spill the beans, and said,

'And John bashes his wife, and that's why Sarah left him, and Lois too. I know heaps of things.'

Javier hung his head; he knew I was right. He seemed to stop verbally abusing my family as much after that. But he kept trying to distance me from my family.

Issues in Javier's family surfaced. For years they'd pointed the finger at Alexandre and accused him of being gay; they'd openly called him a 'maricón', but it got too much for him to take.

Alexandre had had enough of suffering their abuse. After a big argument where all the older brothers ganged up on him, saying he was gay, he screamed out while leaving their house, 'Yes, I am, I admit I'm gay. You have accused me for years; well, I am, and I'm not going to hide it anymore and I'm going.'

Javier and I had just arrived at the house when this argument was on. We heard Alexandre's words as we passed him on his way out but he didn't acknowledge us, getting into his car and leaving. When we went inside, John was fluffing his feathers and telling Javier in Spanish what had happened. All the other brothers were feeding off his aggravation. I was told that they'd just had a fight and Alexandre admitted he was gay; they thought he was upset, but they believed he'd be back.

Days later, when Gema called me, she told me that Alexandre had left the house to live with Gordon, his partner. I was happy for them both. I knew Gordon and he was a great guy. He'd married years ago, but later he discovered he couldn't live a lie. He and his wife had adopted a little girl, but they decided to divorce. Gordon's family learned to accept his sexuality choices and so did his ex-wife, and they became best friends. It never affected their relationship with their daughter, Tanya. This was a normal, understanding family. When I first met Gordon's parents and his ex-wife, Sherry, you could see why. They were all well-adjusted people who understood. Funny, though – Alexandre never admitted to my face that he was gay, and that he and Gordon lived as lovers. I don't know why he acted that way with me.

Javier's family was suffering breakdown, and his father threw a spanner in the works when he started to declare he wanted to go back to Spain to live. To appease him, enough money was raised for him to go back to Spain. Everyone was so happy to get rid of 'the old man', as they called him. But actually, they all fell into disarray, because he was the one who had held them all together with his form of discipline.

So now Javier's father lived in Spain. He wanted his wife to go with him, but she wouldn't leave the boys, deciding to stay in Australia with her sons who clung to her for support and a roof over their heads. Bernat, Vince and Jules never made an effort to improve their lives. With their father gone, they took to drinking at home, whereas they'd never have done that with their father at home. These three were no-hopers wasting their lives and going nowhere fast.

My father-in-law would return to Australia to visit the family. However, when he returned and saw the way they were living, he couldn't stay. His roots were tightly set in Spain. They were glad to get rid of him again. Out of all of us only my son, Julian, missed his grandfather.

Chapter 2

I Find Work

Money became tight for the first time; my sister was working at the Manning factory and she told Javier and me about jobs on the Manning farms, at Summerville. Javier and I discussed the prospect of me working out there. We were used to a standard of living that was declining since he'd taken the job at the pit. His health wasn't as good as it used to be, and he couldn't work long hours anymore. His poor health was an opening for me to venture out of the mundane life of our home, giving me an opportunity to mix with other people. I knew the type of job my sister was telling us about. It wouldn't give me the intellectual stimulation I wanted, but it would give me the freedom I needed. Unfortunately, it would come at a price, I'd soon discover.

I went out to the office on the property. There I spoke to the general manager, who took me to meet one of the individual farm managers, Alex. Alex showed me around the sheds where I'd have to work. I was introduced to one of the women working there. I was in my own world as Alex showed me around the large, long sheds that held hundreds of birds. As I listened to Alex, it all seemed like water off a duck's back for me. I accepted the job and found myself with part-time work. It was by no means a glamourous job, but I was glad to get one. That night I told Javier and it was agreed I could work there.

In June 1981, I started my first job since being married: collecting eggs. It was a hard, dirty job, and the roosters often attacked me when I had my back to them. The chickens were cruel, vicious birds and they pecked me constantly, so I wore a leather arm band to protect my skin from their pecks and scratches. If I startled a chicken in its box, it flew out in self-defence; scratching me madly as it tried to escape the box I was trying to enter with my hand to retrieve its eggs. The chicken would screech, causing the roosters to gang up on me. Many times, I sent a rooster flying into the air with my foot for attacking me. But first I made sure I wasn't being watched.

In the morning I'd make sure the boys were all prepared for school and had all their books and lunches packed for the day. I'd leave them watching TV and they would leave for their bus at 7:30am. It was a big responsibility for them, but Julian was soon turning eleven, so I knew he could handle it. At first, I travelled alone. I didn't mind it, and the solitude in the sheds was equally rewarding. In the quiet of those sheds my mind wandered, and more questions about life surfaced for me to ponder. I was confused about religion, because I never had any religious upbringing. I couldn't bring myself to follow any religion or go along with any religious beliefs.

Marsha was still visiting me and talking to me about the Jehovah's Witness faith; try as I may, I couldn't allow her religion into my life. I was allowing her in my house, though, because of her two daughters, who were school friends of mine. During Marsha's visits, she spoke to me of her eldest daughter and her vanity, and how she couldn't understand her daughter's need to have plastic surgery to improve her appearance. I too couldn't imagine why anyone would want to have their body changed by a surgeon. To me, you are who you are and what you were born with. Nonetheless, Marsha and I had our misunderstanding about other people's need to do things for themselves, outside of our perceptions of what we felt was right. However, Marsha was in my life when I was questioning life. Was she supposed to be in my life? I must say, she was a very patient lady who tried to give me the answers I was seeking, but her answers didn't gel with me. I liked her a lot; Marsha was a soft, warm, friendly-faced lady who gave you the feeling of a real mother's kindness. Knowing her daughters, I could understand why they were so lovely as well.

Time moved on and my days were taken up with working and keeping my house in order. I wanted to break free from Marsha, because my mind was expanding into different fields of thought. She insisted on seeing me after I'd told her at our last visit that I didn't want her to come to my house anymore to talk about religion. I felt her aim was to keep me interested in her beliefs, to try to get me to understand her faith. I remember our last meeting; it was a very hot day. I was in the cool of my home with the air conditioner on. I heard the doorbell ring; on answering it, it was Marsha, and she was so hot. But something came over me to refuse her entry into my home.

I said, 'I don't want to see you today.'

She said, 'But it's very hot today – can I come in for a while?'

Standing my ground, I said, 'No, not today.'

She was upset with me and said, 'I hope one day someone tells you this and doesn't allow you in the cool of their house, then you'll know how I feel.' I was shocked by her words, but I didn't want her to come into my house. I'd been telling her that I wasn't interested in her religion for a long time. I felt bad and said, 'I am sorry.' She turned from my front door and left. I never saw her again. I liked her so much, but I didn't want to listen to her beliefs anymore. About six months later I heard she'd died of cancer. I felt so bad that I'd rejected her from my life.

Not long after this, we lost our beloved dog Laddie. The boys liked to go bike riding to their cousin's house and play there. Laddie always accompanied them. He was so close to Jerod, and I think he loved Jerod the most. This day the boys had gone to look at the neighbour's small creek that flowed through their property. The river was flooded due to some heavy rain we'd had. The neighbours' house was directly across from our house but set back on the property. These people kept to themselves. They ran a taxi business.

The small river had a bridge over it; it was really lovely how they'd had the land set out. Jerod and his brother had gone to investigate the river. But Jerod had decided to come home, and he hadn't called Laddie. He left Laddie with Julian. But Laddie must have noticed

Jerod was gone, and he tore across the road after him. He was hit by a car driving down the main road.

Julian came screaming around to the backyard. I ran out of the house, asking him what was wrong. He told Jerod and me what had happened. As we talked, Laddie ran down Mrs Delmore's property and around to our back gate. He'd run over forty yards and dropped at our feet.

Laddie's love for us was so great. We all screamed with sadness for our beloved dog. He was lying at our feet with his tongue hanging out of his mouth – he was dying. But he'd run to us, to be with us in his death.

The people who'd hit him had come onto our property. The man and his girlfriend carried Laddie to their car and took us all to the nearest vet. All the way to the vet we nursed Laddie and cried uncontrollably for our dog. The man and his girlfriend were so upset for us.

The vet immediately cleared his table and placed our Laddie on it. He tried to help him, but he was sorry; Laddie had a broken back and there was nothing he could do for him. Laddie had to be put down. The man who hit Laddie described to the vet how the dog had run a long distance to us, and the vet was amazed that the dog had a broken back and did that.

We all said our goodbyes to Laddie, the boys and I, and he was put down. We had him brought home to be buried in our backyard under the elm tree. My grief was so great for Laddie. I didn't get past it for a long, long time, and I've never forgotten this dog's love for us. His death affected me so much; his love was so strong, and so was his devotion.

Chapter 3

A Tragic Death Hits The Family

Death hit our family through a young member whom I'd never met personally, but whom Mum and Dad knew very well. My cousin Dylan died at the age of thirty-one. Dylan was a bit of an adventurer and he loved to travel. He'd made many journeys overseas. His passion was my passion. One day, I hoped that Javier and I would travel and live in different countries for periods of up to two months or more. I often suggested that we travel when the boys were off our hands, but he never really answered me.

Dylan had gone to Zimbabwe, in Africa, in 1982. He and the group of people he was travelling with were attacked; if they were killed, their bodies were never found. His parents, Kim and Conrad, were devastated; they couldn't accept his death. Especially having no body returned to them. Dad felt that the bodies would have been so badly mutilated that the authorities may have said that they weren't able to find them. I remembered Dylan's sister Peggy. We'd met her once or twice. Dylan's death brought Dad's first cousin, Conrad, closer to him. Both Conrad and Kim seemed to rely on Dad, with Mum and Dad visiting them more often.

Africa always had a dark side to it for me. Dylan's death seemed to make it darker. But I was still mystified by Africa.

Chapter 4

Having To Fit In

Bianca fell pregnant again with her fourth child. At least she and Conrad seemed to be getting on really well. They'd moved to Eddington; there they were renting a lovely home. When Bianca was with Henry in Pottersville, she always thought her home was too far away from the family. Bianca and the younger family members needed to be close to the main family home where their mother was.

Conrad got her a house in Eddington, for her to be closer to her mother and sisters. This made it easy for her to get help. But she suffered from a lot of mental anguish; I didn't know why, and Gema didn't know why either. Bianca's health was getting worse, and she'd lost a lot of weight. Months later all would be revealed: after having Shelly she'd become more ill. It was found out that she had developed a disease to do with her red blood cells; I'd never heard of it. However, I learned sickle cell disease is mostly found in the Black races. It confirmed to me that there had to have been a Moor influence in their family lineage. I was intrigued.

On my side of the family, my mother had a Chinese lineage. Families were really fascinating to me – their makeup and the many cultures that can be in a family lineage. It showed me where families started. This fascinated me so much and gave me more questions to ponder.

While working on the farms, I was moved around, and I had to interact with the ladies on these different farms. When I was placed on a new farm, I met new ladies who'd come from the Denver Shire and they allowed me to travel with them. This was good. I was ready to share and carpool. But this carpooling came at a price. I was very good with my word knowledge at that time from reading books, and I was starting to use a better vocabulary. As I travelled with these ladies and talked with them, they started to make fun of the way I spoke and of the conversations I liked to engage in. Their jeering became unbearable. I had two choices – either I left their company and travelled alone, or I changed my ways to suit them. I decided to change my ways. I said to them, 'If I can't beat you, I'll join you.' They laughed, and I never talked to them about anything that was 'highbrow', as they referred to me, and my neighbour Mrs Delmore had informed me: I was being 'highbrowed'.

They were happy. I believed they felt a sense of relief, because I wasn't bringing up topics that were too difficult for them to handle. Our trips to work and home were better from then on – we all got on okay. I found out they weren't interesting people. They were happiest when they gossiped. Their conversations were beyond me, as far as gossip goes. I've never liked gossip; my neighbour was also into it. She loved to gossip about people in the town. I had no idea of who she was speaking about, who they were or what their lives were like. Such things didn't interest me, and I tried to figure out why these people found so much joy in running others down.

So the trips were quiet on my behalf, though I'd make an occasional comment. After a while I found my speech became affected and I was losing my ability to pronounce words properly; this was due to virtually being told not to speak with the words I was using, because 'you're too highbrowed for us'. I tried to deal with this inability to pronounce words properly. It's amazing how their low-level use of words affected me and how the lack of using stimulating words starting to affect my ability to speak properly. I questioned myself: can this really happen? Now and then I'd start a conversion with the manager of the farm, and the ladies would look at me as if to say, *Look, there she goes again, being highbrowed.*

During this time, a really lovely lady came to work with us, and her name was Sue. Sue was so nice. We got on so well. She was a like-minded person. Our friendship grew and I found out she was part Aboriginal, which intrigued me. She too had that lovely milky brown-coloured skin like my Uncle Pete, who was part Aboriginal. But his parents were so dark-skinned, there must have been a throwback in him or some white lineage intervention.

Sue loved to knit jumpers and she'd bring her knitting in and knit at work to fill in her break times. There was something I really liked about Sue; I could see she was a very creative person, and many of the sweaters she knitted she was doing from her own mind, not from a pattern. I felt a special kind of energy around her.

One day in the shed, Sue and I accidentally touched hands. It was amazing, the electricity that went through the pair of us. We looked at each other, but the other workers were there, and we made no comment. Sue invited me over to her house in Roma Meadows so we could form a friendship apart from work, to talk about the things we liked to discuss. We loved to talk about the unknown, and she told me she could help me to understand what I was seeking in life.

So I asked Javier if I could go and visit Sue. He asked me a hundred and one questions about her. I answered him as much as I could. He agreed for me to go and visit her, only if he could come with me. The day came when we'd agreed to meet. I wanted her friendship badly, but alone, not with Javier. However, he either came or I wasn't allowed to go. So he came with me to her home in Roma Meadows.

As soon as Sue saw him at the door with me, her whole persona changed. I said to her as I watched her face changing, 'I hope you don't mind, but Javier wanted to come to meet you.'

Shocked, she said, 'No, come in,' but she didn't approve. It was a difficult time for both of us and we couldn't speak on the topics we wanted to talk about. We ended up listening to Javier talk to us.

After that incident Sue never invited me to her home again, and not long after that she left the farms. I lost contact with her. I learned too late that sometimes it's better not to tell Javier everything. Regardless, I couldn't do that; I was too honest, and I had to tell him.

There were times when I did tell white lies – these were to get me and the boys out of trouble in the home over some trivial incident.

Not long after this, Julian was playing near the clothesline and fell onto the handle, and a massive lump formed on the back of his head. He was okay. I was telling Mrs Delmore about the incident, and she told me to be careful with Julian, that he could develop a tumour. The word 'tumour' freaked me out and I nearly experienced a blackout in front of her. Everything seemed to spin away from me. It was as if all voices were being spoken to me from a distance. It took me a while to return from the shock of her words. All I could hear was Mrs Delmore calling to me. I came back to where I was. She was concerned and apologised for upsetting me. I told her that it was alright, her words had just brought up some fear around one of my children being seriously hurt or badly affected by an injury.

I noticed from that experience, and the experiences with the ladies at the farm, that I was slowly losing my speech and my ability to pronounce my words properly. I was suffering from a speech deficiency. I couldn't pronounce my words, which brought about more humiliation from my boys. Did I suffer a shock that had affected a part of my brain? I had blacked out slightly.

Chapter 5

Mind Games That
Javier Delights In

The boys missed Laddie, so we decided to get another dog. We were coming home from a day's trip to Rosemont and Jerod spotted a pet shop, so Javier pulled the car over. Jerod was so excited. We all got out of the car and strolled into the pet shop. Inside, we looked at the puppies. Jerod immediately chose one; it was the cutest puppy, with a very pretty face, and it looked so quiet, as if it was the quietest of the litter. Jerod picked her up; he wanted her there and then. We tried to get him to get a boy dog, but no, he wanted this one. The pet shop owner helped Jerod by convincing us it was best to get a girl dog. He suggested we either have her de-sexed before she turned five months old or let her have a litter of pups. He said that a girl dog makes a good pet, that they were cleaner and didn't have nasty-smelling urine. We agreed, and the puppy was snuggling into Jerod – it was obvious that it was love at first sight. So this puppy came home with us. In the car, she was so quiet and never said boo. As we drove home, we tried to invent a name for her. I suggested Candy and the boys liked that, so that was her name.

Well, she had us bluffed. That night she played up holy hell and became trouble ever since she stepped into our world. Candy had a strong will. No one was telling her what to do. She was so much trouble and full of mischief. One day on returning from an outing, we found her hanging on the cyclone wire fence from her back leg; she'd gotten her leg caught in the fence as she'd tried to escape the yard. She was always trying to escape us, or she just had a wild nature that was suppressed and needed to be free. Now I see that Jerod had picked his own mother. When we released Candy from the fence, we took her over to the vet. He said she had a torn ligament and had to wear a plaster cast. None of us could ever get close to this dog – not that she growled at us. She was just a distant dog and didn't want to be domesticated at all. Nonetheless, we loved her and never mistreated her, and we did the best we could for her well-being.

In 1982, we got a video player. The boys liked *The Chinese Boxer, Midnight Express,* and *Jaws,* and we really liked Clint Eastwood movies. In later years we followed the *Police Academy* movies. The video player brought some laughter and entertainment into our lives. But it wasn't enough entertainment to stop Javier using me for his personal enjoyment, inflicting torments on me that only caused tensions between us, especially as the boys were getting older.

An incident in our neighbourhood had shown me a side to Javier I'd not seen before. The dogs in the neighbourhood were barking and we were investigating the reason why. As we looked out the window, we saw the neighbours who owned the taxi business standing on the main road speaking to some people, who had strayed onto their land. Often people would venture onto their land because it looked like a park, with the river running through it and weeping willows draping into the edge of the river. They were probably explaining to these people that it was private property. I'd heard they didn't like people going onto their property, and fair enough; after all, it was their home.

Julian told us sometimes he and Jerod liked to go and look at the ducks and the other water creatures that gathered there. I understood Julian wanting to go and see the ducks. But I explained to him that it was the neighbours' private property and he probably shouldn't go on it. I know the boys had been on it, because when they went to see the ducks, Laddie had missed Jerod and run after him, and that was when he was hit by a car and later died.

We'd sat down, and suddenly Javier stood up. For no apparent reason, he must have been fuming internally over what Julian explained to us, how he liked to visit their river. Out of the blue Javier screamed out, 'If those people or anyone hurts my kids, I'll avenge them.'

We looked at Javier. I thought, *He must think these people would hurt our boys.* Pausing in shock, I said, 'You can't be vengeful to other people. Somehow you have to go past it – revenge isn't the answer.'

He was more upset and screamed at me, saying, 'If someone killed your son, you'd not kill them back?'

I moved in my seat because I felt threatened and stated, 'No, Javier, I wouldn't.' I think if he could have killed me, he would have.

I had no idea about forgiveness in those days, and my heart wasn't full of malice. I did understand revenge was not the answer. Although I felt no malice towards people, my hatred was growing inside me, because of where I'd put myself. I knew Javier was protective, and he'd defend his children. But revenge was not the answer. Some days were unbearable, and because Javier had an audience, he tormented as much as he could. However, when he started to put his nonsense into the boys' heads that was when I objected. Javier and his friend Len were always dreaming up nonsense around political issues. He was creating hatred and bigotry. I'd had this drilled into my head as a child, and I didn't want the boys to grow up with other people's biases. To Javier and Len, the Americans were the problem and the Russians had the right idea – communism was the way to go, and damnation to the Jews. These crappy ideas were coming from his friend Len; Javier had no political interest before he met Len.

What I was against was his bigoted ways. Now I was faced with bigots again. I tried to voice my concerns about his actions by saying, 'Don't tell the boys these things; let them develop their own opinions.' However, he became more enraged, because I'd told him in front of the boys not to voice his opinions. But they weren't his opinions.

My rage was so great it upset my speech, which caused me to develop more impediments. I wasn't able to get my words out properly. I was losing the ability to express myself. I knew what bigotry could do to people.

Sometimes my boys laughed at me. I was so lost and downtrodden. I was losing the boys' respect as well. Javier would lash out and tell me to mind my own business, to not put him down in front of his boys. 'I'm not, Javier, I am just asking you to let them work it out for themselves,' I'd tried to say, but Javier was as thick as a brick. The more I objected, the more he taunted me. I was just as bad for reacting, but I knew what it was like to have young fertile minds wasted on nonsense. I'm sure he thought I was trying to belittle him; I wasn't. I just didn't like him putting his biased opinions into their young minds.

In my childhood I had listened to such hatred, which confused me, because I couldn't see why people hated others due to the colour of their skin, their religion or beliefs. To me, it was a form of abuse. My reactions were great, and I'd go into a state of screaming. I couldn't tolerate the attitude of a bigot, and Javier knew it. He delighted in his taunts. Once, I accidentally caught him saying to the boys 'Watch this' as I'd turned to say something, and the three of them were laughing.

'Javier, what are you doing?' I asked.

'I'm talking to the boys, not you, and it's got nothing to do with you, it's a joke between us,' he sniggered.

'You're playing games with me, aren't you,' I said with disappointment in my exhausted voice, as if he'd drained every bit of energy from my body.

'Don't be stupid,' he smirked.

I said, 'You think it's funny, Javier, doing these things to me, don't you?'

He then stated, 'You're mad.'

'Yes, I am, and you're madder than me,' I returned, raising my eyebrows. He had a new tactic to play with now, seeing as my family wasn't an issue after me telling him that I knew his family's secrets. Our boys were his weapon he used to upset me.

Even though Javier was cruel, I too could be just as cruel to him with my words.

I remember the day I'd had enough. Javier had worked me up too much and pushed me over my line. He and our boys were laughing at me, and I blurted out, 'Why don't you tell our boys why we're paying six dollars a week to a kid that's yours?' I was so angry with him.

The boys looked at me and everyone stopped. Silence surrounded us. Javier's eyes changed, and he glared at me. Moving in closer, he went to raise his hand. I said, 'Go on, just try it – hit me and I'll call the police, and there's always Mrs Delmore to fall back onto.' I was sick of him looking good in front of Julian and Jerod. Why should I be the bad one all the time? He knew what I meant when I mentioned Mrs Delmore's name, because of the time he chased me with a shotgun; the boys never knew what happened that night.

He turned away from me, snarling at me, backing off as he told the boys to go with him. Like puppy dogs, they followed him. As he walked away, I asked him, 'Why am I here, Javier?' He didn't answer me. I said, 'You're driving me mad and I hate you. You have no idea how much I hate you.'

Many times during these mind games, I reacted very badly, but the mental and emotional games never stopped. Then the silent treatment came. That nearly killed me. We'd wait for someone to come and visit us to break the ice so we could talk again. I hated his mentality, but I also hated silence. I could see his delight in my reactions, but I couldn't control myself and stop reacting. However, this day took the smile off his face, but I never brought it up again.

I grew to hate Javier more and more. I felt trapped, like a bird in a cage; I had no one to tell my problems to. I felt lots of isolation and misunderstanding from him and the boys, and from everyone, for that matter. I would never tell anyone what my life was really like; everyone thought we were the perfect couple and that we never fought, because around our families we never did. While we were at his mother's house, I was always busy with his sisters. In my preoccupation with them, I forgot our bad times in my own house.

I wasn't innocent myself; I had my own issues with my boys. I spoke to them in an abusive way at times. I knew I was doing the wrong thing, but I never enforced my spiritual beliefs on them. I believed that they should discover certain beliefs in life for themselves. Politics, religion, and spirituality – these beliefs could be self-determined later in life. Now, it was important for them to learn constructive information to open their minds, without the biases of bigots, so they could instil beliefs from an educational point of view. This is what I wanted in my own childhood: interesting talks leading to ideas where I could form my own beliefs and impressions of life.

I had my faults too. Impatience when we were out because the boys were shy, and I would become impatient and answer their questions; I tried to give them time and independence, but my concern was not for us, it was for the person waiting for an answer, be it the doctor or teacher.

As time went on, Javier's anger grew stronger; he started to hit me across the face with a rolled-up newspaper, but never with his hand. A couple of times he'd blackened my eyes. The worst thing was that he did this in front of the boys. They seemed locked in fear and couldn't say a thing around their father. It was as if they weren't themselves. Maybe they knew you could only go so far with him. His mind was twisted, and it snapped easily. I think they feared him as much as I did. However, he never hit them. But he'd take the boys down the backyard and talk to them. I don't know what he told them – secrets, I guessed.

Chapter 6

The Past Catches Up, Or Was It A Dream?

I felt uneasy in the house and wondered why Julian had gone to his father's bedroom. There was no light in the bedroom. As I peered up the hallway, I questioned myself – *should I go up there and see what's going on, or shouldn't I worry?* But I was worried – why? I walked quietly up the hallway on soft footsteps, edging my way to the door of the bedroom. I placed my back up against the hallway wall. *Do I enter the bedroom or leave now?* I listened for noises, but I couldn't hear them speaking. I was concerned as I edged to the doorway. I must go in. Like a flash, I put my hand on the bedroom light switch, took it off again and placed my back up against the wall. My heart was racing. Why did I feel this way? 'I must enter this room,' I said to myself. A voice within said, 'No, go in, go in.' I turned the light on. As I dived into the brightly lit room, I saw Julian and his father in bed. They quickly moved apart. I asked, 'What's going on here? What are you doing?' The child jumped up out of the bed and ran away. I woke to realise it was a dream.

My past was surfacing for me to confront it. However, I was not ready to do that. The dream was to do with my own experiences with Dad. But I couldn't deal with those issues. So I pushed the memories back down and buried them deeper in the back of my mind. The flashbacks made me sad. I cried as I agonised – why did this happen to me? And why did Dad do that to me? I was just a child.

The whole experience unfolded in that dream before my eyes – to see myself running from my father's bedroom when Mum had come in unexpectedly and caught my father fondling me. As a child, I had enjoyed his touch and the feelings he offered me. But he caused me pain, deep pain with my mother. I sat up in the bed, shaking the memory away; it was too painful to remember. I knew it was to do with my fears around sexuality, with my own children becoming victims of child molesters. I just hoped they never, ever encountered any of those traumatic experiences.

There were lots of fears in my life, and there was a big fear around my brother Barton. He hardly ever came to visit us, especially when Javier wasn't at home. It was a quiet day and I was washing up after lunch. I'd washed a few dishes and stopped as I saw Barton coming onto my back patio near my kitchen door. As I saw him, fear gripped me. I couldn't understand it, because he was my brother.

Next, I heard, 'Chris, are you home?'

'Yes, Barton, what's wrong?' I asked nervously, making my way to the door, wiping my hands on a tea towel. 'Do you want to come in?' I asked.

'No, mate – can I go to Javier's garage? I want to borrow his welder,' he asked. Relief seized me. I came out of the house and walked over to the garage with him. Barton was in a hurry; he grabbed the welder and left. I don't know why I feared him for that second. The past was resurfacing what I'd buried – anything that reminded me of Dad, causing me to become upset. Maybe I thought I'd buried it, and I hadn't; now it was testing me. I shuddered at the thought of those childhood memories. I was definitely not ready to face those issues of my youth.

It was 1983; Julian had to travel further to school now he was at the Catholic high school in Wentworth. Once again, the religious Brothers had to leave, and they were replaced by lay teachers. Julian had built up a good rapport with the Brothers, and he liked them. The school was renamed St Benedict's High School. It was hard for Julian when I went to his school. Because I looked so young for my age and so much younger than the other boys' mothers, he was asked if I was his biological mother by other students. I was thirty-two and looked as if I was about twenty-two. When Julian told me this, I was surprised, because I never saw myself as young-looking. As a matter of fact, I never saw myself as any age.

To me, age was a number I was up to in life. Julian's friends were commenting and making me aware of my looks, but that was short-lived. I soon forgot how young I looked. I don't think the boys worried so much, like I did with my own mother looking too young. Actually, they seemed to be proud of it. I did wonder why I looked so young.

Chapter 7

Mum's Mum Dies And Family Secrets Are Revealed

My mother's mother died in 1983. Grandma was always Grandma Owens to me, and Mum was Carol Owens. But years ago, when I got my birth certificate, I found out that there was a different name on it. Mum told me that, for legal papers, I had to use the name Henderson.

Mum was devastated by her mum's loss. My brother Barton was always the closest to Mum's mum, more than my father's mother, Grandma Kinread, whom we all lived with. I don't think Grandma Kinread liked Barton as much as she liked Maxine and me, and she made that quite clear.

So Barton had developed a stronger love for Mum's mum. He'd often call in on her and have a chat to check up on her. She'd been unwell with bouts of asthma. It was around 9pm when he called in to see Grandma; her front light was still on as he pulled up in his car, turning off the motor and finishing off his cigarette. Barton alighted from his car, throwing the butt down on the asphalt road and squashing it with his boot. He slowly walked up to her front yard and onto her homemade brick footpath that was adorned by flowerbeds on either side with seasonal flowers. As he walked the path, he felt the house was too still, he told us. His heavy footsteps on the old wooden boards caused them to creak, and he hoped he didn't frighten Grandma. So he sang out, 'Grandma, its Bart, are you awake?'

There was no answer. He called out to her again, a little louder: 'Grandma, it's me, Barton.' There was no response. He became a bit worried and peered through the window. He couldn't see through the white nylon curtains, so he went to the front door and knocked, singing out to Grandma, and then his anxiety grew. In the heat of the moment, he forced the front door open, he told us. In the house, all the rooms were in darkness except for Grandma's bedroom. Edging in there, Barton saw she was propped up on her pillows; he said she looked like she was asleep. 'Grandma, it's Barton,' he timidly called out. He moved in closer and touched her arm, half expecting her to wake up. But she was still, and he realised she'd died.

He said her cold body was stiff to the touch, but her face showed peace and contentment. He gently brushed his hand over Grandma's hair as tears welled up in his eyes. He loved her. He kissed her forehead and said, 'Goodbye, Grandma.' Leaving the house, Barton went next door. He knocked on their door and asked the neighbour to call an ambulance; he did. Barton returned to Grandma and sat with her as he waited for the ambulance to come to take her body away.

He wondered how he was going to break the news to Mum that he found Grandma dead in her bed. He knew it would be hard on Mum to hear of her death.

At my parents' house, Barton called Dad outside to tell him first, and then they both confronted Mum. She took it badly. It was the next day that Barton came over to let me know about my grandma's passing. He told Javier and I that Grandma looked so peaceful, like she was in a deep sleep and resting. He paused and said, 'But as I touched her and gently pushed her arm, she was solid and cold.' Barton was very upset. We all were, but not to the extent he was; he'd sat with her in her death. I guess that must have had some effect on him.

On the day of Grandma's funeral, Javier and I pulled up in our car at the crematorium. I got out of our car. As I glanced over to the building, I could see Mum and Barton. I walked over to them. Mum was beckoning me to come to her, and I could see she really needed me. Javier could see her need for me too. He moved up closer to me and started to physically pull me back. I questioned him with my eyes. He stared even more intensely at me, as if to say, 'Don't you go to her.' So I had to back off.

My brother supported Mum into the service. I felt so bad and cowardly that I had to submit to this man's will. Of all days for him to play up, because Mum really needed me. Javier's glare was too much for me to deal with later on. I looked at Mum to say, 'I can't go to you.' I looked at him from the corner of my eye to indicate why. Javier hated my family so much, but he'd never tell them to their faces. I knew the truth of how he hated them, but he acted so nice around them. They had no idea what this man was really like. He was a gutless wonder, using his sickly smile to make out that he liked my family and I was the problem, not him.

I had a problem, and it was him. But I couldn't leave him; I had the boys and I knew I couldn't provide a good life for them. I wanted them to be educated and to have a chance in life. On my own, I'd never be able to financially support them. I needed him; he was a good provider. I wanted the boys to have the opportunities I never got.

Javier's hatred and jealousy towards my family was unwarranted. I don't know why he was like that, because I never gave him any cause to be jealous of me. All he could do was condemn my family and say I came from a family of liars and sluts. Even in front of our children he verbalised his hatred, which drove me mad. He was the one who was crazy and mad because of his fears of my love towards other people.

Not long after Grandma's death, Mum got a mysterious call from a woman. The woman asked Mum if she was Del's daughter. Mum told her she was. The lady said, 'I'm your half-sister, and you have three other half-sisters and a brother.'

On my next visit, Mum confronted me. She said, 'It's strange, Chris, I got a call from a woman this week.'

Curious, I asked, 'Yes, what did she say?' Mum hesitated in answering my question. I was the one she confided in. She knew she could trust me. She had to tell someone. I think her mum was her second confidant. Now she was gone.

Then she answered me, saying, 'It's strange.'

'I know, Mum, you said that, so what was so strange?'

'I don't know if I should tell you, but I felt I had to. It's Grandma.'

More curious, I encouraged her to tell me with a smile, 'Yes, tell me.' I became a little impatient with her. 'Mum, tell me. You started it, now tell me.'

She blurted out, 'This woman said she was a daughter of Grandma's.'

Surprised, I said, 'Oh! Mum, did you tell her you want to come and see her?'

Mum snapped, 'No, I don't want to see her. She wants to see me, but no. I told her, "Let sleeping dogs lie."'

This was typical of Mum – it was how she dealt with things she couldn't handle. So I expected her to react this way. But she wasn't going to get away with it that easily. I said, 'But Mum, we could get to know more about Grandma.'

This idea infuriated Mum; she didn't want to go down that road. She jumped on me and said, 'No, and that's it.' I knew it was over. I couldn't insist anymore with her. But it left me wondering. After her outburst, I agreed with her to ease her concerns, saying, 'Okay, Mum, let it be.'

My curiosity was great, but so was Mum's inability to face reality. And I still wondered about my grandma. She was such a strange lady; she had two names, and all my life I knew her as Grandma Owens, but when I got older – and if I had to fill in legal documents – I had to write my mum's maiden name as Henderson. Grandma was such a mysterious lady, but by the same token, she was a very independent woman. I admired her independence and remember seeing her up the street paying her bills or shopping. I'd marvel at her. Even being partially blind, she still managed to carry out her own duties. She was nothing like my mum: fragile and timid.

Grandma could never see you as you approached her in the street; you always had to let her know who you were. Often, I'd question why she was so quiet. She never spoke to me much. When I did tell her it was me, she'd say, 'Oh, Christine.' I felt no love from her, and I wondered: did she dislike me?

Life hadn't been kind to Mum's mum, and it'd never been easy for Mum either. Mum didn't have many people to confide in, only me. She was upset over the loss of her mother, but she told me she was more upset over the loss of my Grandma Kinread, which surprised me. I wondered why, after all the mistreatment she'd gotten from Grandma Kinread. I'd look at Mum, thinking, 'How could you be sad over her loss, when she was so cruel to you?'

As if Mum was reading my mind, she explained, 'Chris, when your Grandma Kinread died, she and Grandfather Kinread came to my bed.'

My ears pricked up. 'Mum…'

'Yes, they both were so young and beautiful.' She paused, and looked up at me and said, 'Chris, they wanted me to join them on the other side.'

Startled, I said, 'But you can't, Mum, until it's your time to go over.'

She calmly said, 'I know, but they were beckoning me to come. I said to them both, "I can't go yet; I have to look after Max." When I looked at your dad and looked back at them, they'd gone. They never came back to me again.'

I asked, 'Were you afraid to see them?'

She replied, 'No, I had no fear about seeing them. They both looked so happy and at peace.'

Whenever Mum confided in me, I could see it was a load off her mind. I was happy that she was approached by my grandparents. I too knew there was another side to life. Mum's actions made me wonder why she wasn't fearful of the other side, when she feared life on this side so much. It was strange – I didn't fear life on this side; even though I knew of the other side, I feared it only because I had no knowledge on it. I had felt the other side in our old house. So why did I fear something I knew existed? And why was it that human beings feared both sides? I knew we were watched over at our farmhouse. I was frightened of the invisible in the two bottom rooms; funny, though, never in the rest of the house, where we mainly lived. It was as if they'd separated our house, and there were two different spaces in time in that same house.

Chapter 8

Escaping The Normality Of Our Lives

We did lots of home renovations with the extra money from my job, and we were now back on track money-wise. Our improvements made our house a real picture amongst the older houses in our street. As we improved our house, so did our neighbours. They painted their houses and started to tend to their lawns. Especially Mrs Delmore, who had never had her lawn, mowed all the time we lived there. It was good to see these improvements. We put up a new fence around the house to allow us more privacy. It cut out Mrs Delmore's and my chatting over the back fence. But I chatted to her in the front yard, and I often chatted to my neighbours if I saw them in their front yards. Now I was working, I didn't visit them.

We had a lovely wrought-iron fence put up around the front yard, and had a landscaper come in. He set up a low-maintenance garden for us, full of hardy Australian shrubs and plants. We put a large Bomanite concrete slab, twenty-by-twenty-foot patio out the back near the kitchen door. We put up a double-layered fibreglass wall sealed with plants and shells to give a seaside effect along Mrs Delmore's side. Now we enjoyed more outdoor activities and had barbecues more often in the spring and summer times. This patio actually cooled our house down, and we had the landscaper put a garden around it as well.

Things were very good on the financial side of life, so much so that in 1984, we decided to go on a South Pacific cruise around the islands, rather than go caravanning, which we had done every school holiday since Jerod was a baby.

Javier had agreed to my proposal that we take a cruise that year. So we put down a deposit and paid it off. We chose a Christmas cruise, December 1984, returning home just before New Year's Eve. When we booked the cruise with our local travel agent, she suggested that we take a cabin in the centre of the ship because there were stabilising bars to prevent seasickness there, and we'd feel less movement in the ship, so we agreed to her advice.

Our marriage was dead as far as I was concerned. I just bore with it until the boys were older, then I was going to leave Javier. But I think Javier never believed I would actually leave him. The boys' lives were important to me. I wanted them to have a good start in life with good foundations to help them create a better life for themselves. I reasoned that their education was paramount to ensure a good life. In our family we had no university-trained family members; this had to stop with my boys.

The day came to go away. The weather that year was terrible; it was still cold in December. We drove to

Rosemont and parked our car, making our way to the ship. After checking in, we boarded the cruise liner. We were escorted down the corridor to our cabin. As we moved into the belly of the boat, I freaked out, because there were no windows, only a narrow walkway.

I grabbed Javier's arm. Fear gripped me. He asked me, 'What's up?'

Stunned, I said, 'I can't stay here, there's no windows. Javier, please, I have to leave.'

'It's okay, come on,' he insisted, as he took my hand.

We made it to our cabin door. It was in a tight little narrow annex. The cabin steward told us that he'd forgotten our key. He walked off.

'Javier, I can't stay here, I'll die.'

'It's okay. What's got into you?' he asked. Terror was in my eyes. I had no idea why I was so frightened in this narrow walkway. While waiting for the steward, I became more claustrophobic, then I tried to run back out of the small annex, but Javier grabbed me, telling me to calm down. The steward returned with the key. He quickly opened the door. As soon as I saw the porthole, I was alright.

On our first day out to sea, I became very seasick. I was laid up for two days in the cabin. I felt so bad, because Javier was so nice to me. Prior to the trip I was mean. I'd coldly told them that if anyone got sick, they shouldn't expect me to miss out on my holiday looking after them. And it was me who suffered. Boy, oh boy, did I suffer. But I never expected them to stay indoors with me. As soon as I slept, they went off. After the second day I was fine and got my sea legs.

On the cruise, we met a lovely English couple, Judy and Hugh, and we befriended them. They had four children, ranging from eight to fifteen, so my boys made friends with their children. But Judy told us they suffered with sleepless nights due to the motion of the ship, because they'd had a cabin on the bow. When they took us to their cabin, sure enough, it was very bad. It was a lovely big cabin, but the motion was terrible. Now we understood what the travel agent meant about movement. Our cabin was small but stable.

The cruise was so relaxing; the children were off most of the day doing their thing, and we all went to bed around 3am and got up at 9am for the morning activities. I felt the cruise was very safe for our boys, and there were lots of families there with children who were also running around freely.

Because I hated Javier, I didn't care what he did. I did notice a young girl hanging around him. One afternoon she'd come from nowhere and asked Javier to help her with her stereo. He asked me if he could go. I brushed him off to go with her. I think I was so unhappy with him I never reasoned it out in my mind. I'd have done anything to get rid of him for a few hours and that was all I was interested in.

As I write this memory out, I can remember her face as clearly as if I saw her yesterday. She had a look of wanting him. But I just dismissed the whole thing. 'Go, go,' I said. They left; I didn't even watch them go away. I went and did my own thing, walking around the ship and looking in the shops. I was free to do what I wanted. Not that that lasted for too long. Javier was soon back and close by me. As I spent my time walking around the shops, I spotted some Lladró ornaments. I told Javier I wanted to buy some. He allowed me to buy them. I also bought myself a garnet ring.

There was also another girl interested in Javier, and she was part of the variety show. She actually looked like Javier's sister Gema. She for sure had a crush on Javier – I could see it. But to be truthful, I just didn't care. If he left me, better still. I secretly wished for some other woman to come and take him away from me, because I knew if I left him, I'd have nothing, so he had to go himself for us to benefit.

Javier was highly sexual. It was terrible because when he wanted sex, he got it, even when the boys were sharing a confined space with us, be it this cabin or even when we went caravanning. He didn't care; when his urge rose up, he wanted sex. He had to have it and I had to give it to him. Jerod always seemed to be awake when Javier was in that mood. When he was younger, on one of our caravanning trips before we got the boys beds to sleep on in the annex, Jerod asked us if we were finished. I was really angry with Javier, but he still didn't care. I hated his attitude, because to me he had no respect for our boys or me. If I refused him, there would be a fight, so I couldn't win.

When we came back from the cruise, I really liked travelling and suggested to Javier that we save our money for another trip and go to New Zealand. We could do a self-driving trip around the two islands. He agreed, so we saved. I was starting to have the urge to travel.

I planned more travel, but a problem occurred. We never went on any more trips outside of Australia, because Javier injured himself at work. He fell, hurting his back. Now he was off work for a long period of time. I kept working, and gradually he seemed to recover, returning to work on light duties, which didn't work out for him. So he had to go off work and stay home on his own.

To occupy himself he decided to buy a bird. He set up the bird's cage near the back garage and brought home a white cockatoo, which we called Jockey. We were told that Jockey was a boy; however, Jockey started to lay eggs, so it was a girl. Javier had Jockey's wings clipped so he could let her out of her cage to walk around on the grass. The first time Javier pulled her out of her cage, he must have hurt her, or the bird just didn't like him at all. From then on, as soon as the bird was out of the cage, she squawked and raised her crest, chasing Javier around the yard and trying to nip at him.

When Javier was away, I would get Jockey out of the cage. She actually loved me so much. If I lay out in the sun on the back lawn, she'd come and smooch into my face and kiss me. She really did love me. I'm not sure if she had sympathy for me and understood the cruel nature of Javier. I was not a bird lover; her love was greater for me than mine for her. Nonetheless, I allowed her to kiss me.

If Javier came home unexpectedly and Jockey was out, I'd have to quickly put her back into her cage. As I did this, she would move her tongue back and forth, making a sound as if she was trying to talk to me and smooch into me.

Having her in the cage distressed me. I told Conrad, Bianca's partner, about Jockey and he asked his parents, who loved animals like their own kids, if they would take her, and they did. So we gave Jockey to Bianca's mother-in-law. I was happy for Jockey, because their family allowed her to live in their house and walk wherever she wanted to go; she was free.

With Javier's injury, we had to go to many specialist doctors and to the solicitor. I always had to accompany him because he had no education, and sometimes he couldn't understand what the doctors or solicitors were saying to him. So I had to translate for him. Some of our trips involved visiting Rosemont to see specialists for further opinions. I don't think Javier trusted himself. After visiting the solicitor, he'd ask me what the man had said. I'd explain it all to him, what was said and required of him. In regard to legal matters, he couldn't function without me.

It was a trying time; however, there I found a message for me. While visiting one of these doctor's surgeries, I came across a magazine with a fishing village in it. This scene sparked something inside me. I had to go there. I said to Javier, 'When our boys are grown up and leave us, we can go travelling and live in different countries for a couple of months.' He wasn't interested and just said, 'We could.' But I knew he wouldn't. That photo stayed in my mind, and somehow, I had to get there.

Fighting was the only time we really talked. I hated Javier even more now he was at home. I had to tread carefully and watch every word I said, because he easily misinterpreted what I said, and he'd become more upset. I was glad I still had my job four days a week; even though it was a dirty job, it helped me keep my sanity. Plus, we needed it to supplement Javier's compensation.

I was so glad we got to achieve all we did before his accident: doing our house up and having that cruise – it was so worthwhile. All our hard work paid off. It was rewarding when I assessed where we were in regard to our personal comforts. But the future worried Javier, and when he was concerned, I'd say, 'Don't worry, it will all work out in the end.' It always did. I never had a fear for our future; it was going to be okay.

When Javier saw me thinking, he'd ask me, 'What are you thinking about?'

'Nothing, nothing at all,' I'd tell him, keeping a noncommittal face. He became more paranoid, insisting on finding out what was going on in my head. I'd ask him when he questioned me, 'Why are you asking me this? I am just relaxing.' And I'd try to keep calm and smile to show him I wasn't upset. But he'd stare at me. I'd look elsewhere or go into the yard and do some work out there. What annoyed me the most was that he could never go to his medical or legal appointments on his own; I had to go with him.

Another incident out of many incidents: I wasn't feeling good and felt some uneasiness coming over me. It seemed to be flowing through my body as I was watching TV with the boys and Javier. The phone rang. As Javier moved towards the phone to pick it up, I said, 'There's been a death.' He stopped and looked at me. He didn't comment on my remark. He answered the phone and it was his brother, Dante, from Chester Hills. They were talking in Spanish.

When Javier got off the phone, he said, 'Dante said that Nita's mother died not long ago.' I looked at him knowingly, but I didn't say anything. After his conversation with Dante, he'd forgotten the remark I'd made earlier. What Javier didn't understand, he ignored. I think deep down he knew what I'd said, but he didn't know how to treat me. Deep down, I knew things; I had an inner knowing. I also didn't fully understand what I knew. But as soon as I found out there had been a death, that strange feeling left me. I felt I was in a living death, living there with him.

Thinking of Nita, I asked Javier, 'How's Nita taking it?'

He replied, 'I don't know.'

I said, 'But Dante must have said how Nita was.'

'No, he didn't, but we'll go to Chester Hills for the funeral,' he stated. No more was said, and we continued to watch our movie as if it were nothing; death cometh and death taketh, and so be it.

Chapter 9

Julian Becomes A Man

We bought Julian his first car when he turned sixteen and he loved it; it was a VW. Javier and I took turns to teach him to drive it. I was so glad he had his own car; that meant freedom. The boys developed a real closeness to me as they got older and confided in me. I think it was because of the freedom I'd pushed them into. We'd spend hours laughing. I was often invited into their rooms so we could talk before they slept. I loved those times with the boys. However, Javier didn't like it. He would come to their bedroom doors to investigate what we were up to. When he entered the room, we stopped talking, then he'd leave us.

I was a free-thinking, open-minded mother. I knew the boys were becoming more sexually active. There was no way of stopping them. I think Jerod had already started on the cruise we'd been on. Anyhow, I wanted my boys to be free-minded and never feel constricted. It was a wonderful bond we had. However, for Javier, this wasn't easy; as the boys got older, Javier started to act strangely. Sometimes his reactions were felt by me and crossed over into the boys' lives as well. I felt his behaviour was out of jealousy, because the boys were always talking to me. We were relating to each other, and I had been growing up with them – there were only nineteen years between Julian and me. Our closeness scared Javier.

I felt it was my turn to have the boys' confidence and attention. Javier had power over them in their younger years, for too long. They were feeling trust with me, and I was protecting them as much as I could and allowing them to be themselves. They knew who to come to when they needed certain advice or to talk on a certain topic.

Drugs were an issue in our community, but I had this lovely rapport with the boys that allowed me to ask them any questions without fear of backlash. They knew I wasn't judging them or reprimanding them; I was curious about their lives and well-being. I asked the boys if they used drugs, because we'd received a newsletter from their school informing us that some students had been caught selling drugs on the school grounds, and that these students were expelled. Jerod told me he knew about the problem and what was going on at school, and he'd told me they were available, but he wasn't interested in taking drugs; Julian likewise. I trusted Jerod and Julian. Julian for sure wouldn't take drugs, because he was too body-conscious and heavily into physical fitness. It was a full-time obsession at home. Football was his love and he trained hard. Julian was gifted with a natural, well-formed body that looked like he was in the gym every day, but he never went to a gym then. He had a few weights at home that Javier made for him, and he did football training. Julian was so much like my side of the family – well-developed before our time.

When Julian turned sixteen, I told him I trusted him as an adult, and it was time for him to make his own decisions about what he wanted to do. I felt I couldn't tell him what to do anymore; the only thing I asked of him was that he returned that trust I had in him. And he did. If he wanted to go to the doctor on his own, he went alone; his privacy was respected. And the same went for Jerod at sixteen. They both agreed with my decision. However, I let them both know I was always there for them. They already knew that, and I knew they knew I'd always listen to them.

Julian really loved his freedom, and having a car was just an added bonus. At the age of fifteen, Julian had had his first beer while we were in Queensland on one of our caravanning holidays. I remember it well: I walked out of the caravan and saw Julian with a beer in his hand. Javier said, 'It's time for him to have a beer.'

I said, 'I agree; after all, he's fifteen.' I think Jerod started to drink a bit earlier; and why not – if they liked a beer, let them have one. It was better than them drinking behind our backs. I'd much rather them enjoy a beer in freedom than sneaking and drinking obsessively because they weren't allowed to.

Jerod had a lovely girlfriend at fifteen, Penny. She was seventeen and so sweet. She used to come over to our house to visit Jerod. On one of her visits, she asked, 'Chris and Javier, can Jerod come to the club with me?'

We looked at each other. Javier didn't comment, and I said, 'I am so sorry, Penny – it's not that we don't want Jerod to go with you to the club. We'd like him to go with you. It's that if he gets caught, he's underage and there'd be trouble due to that.' We had to say no to Penny's request and Jerod understood. Penny did too, but not long afterwards they broke up. I talked to Jerod about the break-up and apologised that we couldn't allow Penny to take him to the club. He was sad but he understood. Jerod seemed to be the one to have his heart broken in his younger life.

It was such a great time when the boys were in their teens, because Javier and I actually got to spend time with their mates and girlfriends. I loved them, and both Javier and I got on so well with their friends. The only downfall was that we became attached to their girlfriends, too.

Jerod got on really well with Milly, Reece and Mike's mum. These brothers' mum was also open-minded. Milly believed in her boys being free to experience life. Reece and Mike lived in Denver Shire. So did Julian's friends Mike and Pete. They all attended the same Catholic high school. Their mates came from all around our surrounding districts. It was a wonderful time, seeing the boys having such a great social life and going out in a group. Jerod was always invited. Julian was seeing him as a friend. Not that they didn't fight – they still fought, because Julian was a first-class torment, and Jerod was a good fish who took the bait all the time. However, when it came time for them to go out, they both changed their attitudes towards each other. Apparently, they got on great outside of the house, and they were both having a drink and I guess this put them in a good mood.

I'll always remember the house was abuzz as they prepared to go out to the local disco. Our moments were fun, especially if Javier wasn't home and I could be cheeky with them. I asked Jerod, 'Have you got your little raincoats?' as he was leaving the house, because I knew he was up to mischief with the glint he had in his eye, and he'd been talking to me about a girl he really liked.

'Little raincoats, Mum? I have to tell you they're big ones.'

I laughed. 'Oh, Jerod, okay, big ones then.' 'Raincoats' was our name we had for condoms.

I really enjoyed my time with my boys at this stage of their lives. We shared so much, and mostly I loved their free, open minds and jokes. I felt their freedom and I wanted them to experience their lives to the fullest.

Sometimes, in Javier's deranged moments that could happen suddenly, he'd flare up for no reason at all. I have no idea why he'd suddenly think in a certain way. We were all free in our thought at this stage of our lives and we were pretty happy in each other's company. But he seemed edgy often.

On an outing to Dawson Hill with Julian, Javier suddenly and for no reason at all attacked Julian verbally; it happened when we were crossing over the train track on Smith Road going into Dawson Hill. He drove off onto the side of the road, stopped the car and told Julian to get out of it. I was stunned. So was Julian.

I said, 'Javier, what's up? He's done nothing.' But something triggered in Javier's brain to upset him. He began to scream at Julian and was telling him to get out of the car. I lashed out back at him and said, 'If he goes, I go too.' So he told us both to get out of the car. We did. He left us standing there.

Julian started to cry. Although he was six foot one and had a natural body any bodybuilder would envy, he was still sensitive and gentle with a kind heart. He said, 'Mum, I don't know what I did.'

Looking at him and his gentle face, I reassured him, 'It's not you. Don't worry, Julian, you did nothing wrong. You know what your father's like; he goes off at the smallest thing.' I would never let my sons down, and I would always support them. We decided to walk to the main street, which was only five minutes' walk away. As we were walking and talking, Javier pulled up next to us, telling us to get back into the car.

He never hit the boys, but he abused them mentally and emotionally at times. All I wanted was to protect them at all costs. Our lives were hell at times. I tried to keep the harmony as much as I could.

This all happened when Julian was quite happy in his life. He was going out and had lots of great mates and girlfriends. Maybe Javier didn't like it, or maybe it brought out his jealousy because of the freedom Julian was having. But he could have left.

At sixteen, Julian was doing Asian Studies at high school. While doing these studies, a wonderful opportunity was given to him and his classmates. They were able to go to Bali for a school excursion. I was elated that he could go. This experience opened him right up. The class was lucky. They had a very modern teacher, Mr Long. I felt Mr Long wanted to give his students a memorable time. Julian loved it over in Bali. He didn't want to come home, he told us when he called us. I understood completely why when he explained the idyllic, slow lifestyle of the Balinese people.

Julian hated the pressures and stresses of everyday life and some of the requirements demanded of him. While in Bali, he and the other boys were mucking around in the swimming pool and he was knocked accidentally up against the pool wall, breaking his front tooth in half.

He was taken to a dentist there and the dentist told him he could wait until he got back to Australia to have it repaired because the nerve wasn't damaged. When he rang to tell us about the incident, we were concerned, but he wasn't. He just loved his time over there. He told me excitedly, 'Mum, I don't want to come home.' I laughed and told him I understood. This opened Julian's life to a love of travel to the Southeast Asian countries in later life.

Chapter 10

The Past Can Repeat Itself

In 1987, in the months of February to March, I couldn't stop thinking about my grandma and the death of her oldest son Donny, and how he died at age of seventeen. The words 'life is a cycle' kept coming through my mind. As I thought about these words, I became more fearful. *Will my oldest child be taken from me?* These feelings got stronger and stronger as the months went by. I knew there was no way to prevent this happening. I had to just wait it out and take it as it came. I didn't tell my children or Javier about these thoughts. I never confided in anyone. I always worked through my issues alone.

However, I needed to talk to someone, so I said to Mum, 'Mum, I feel uneasy, like there's going to be a death. You know how Grandma lost her son? I feel I will lose Julian.'

With horror on her face and bewilderment at my words to talk about my own son like that, she stated, 'Oh, Christine, how could you think that?'

I said to her, sincerely worried, 'Mum, I'm not intentionally thinking this, it's coming through. I don't want you to condemn me for my thoughts, but I'm talking to you to be understood.' I paused. 'I feel it.' Mum assured me that she didn't feel I'd lose Julian. I had to let it go and just wait and see.

It came around to the month of April. I will never forget the day my nephew Alex came to my back door. 'Aunty Chris,' I heard. Whoever it was, they were in trouble. I leaned over the kitchen sink and saw it was Alex. I rushed out to the back door. He was puffing, trying to get his breath; his eyes were nearly bulging out of their sockets. He was on the top step, holding onto the wall for support with one arm, his hand outstretched and his body bent over as he held his chest with his other hand.

Worried, I asked, 'Alex, what's up?'

He said, 'It's okay,' as he tried to breathe.

'No, it's not okay – have you got your puffer?' I enquired.

'Yes,' he said. Alex struggled as he took another breath and asked, 'Have you seen Mum?'

'No, Alex, I haven't,' I said. 'Come into the house and wait here for her.'

He wouldn't; he straightened up, held his chest, and went back down the steps. He seemed in a desperate hurry to find his mother, my sister Maxine. In those days, there was no way to contact anyone unless they were at home, and near a landline. He gradually walked to the end of the house. I asked again, 'Alex, are you alright?' as he got nearer to the corner of the house.

'Yes. I need Mum.' He paused as he looked up the driveway, saying, 'I'll go back home. I am okay.'

'Do you have your puffer?'

He reached into his pocket, bent on leaving me, and pulled out his puffer to show me. There was nothing I could do to stop him. He went off around the corner of the house and out of my sight.

Not long after that incident, Alex had another bad asthma attack. Again, he was rushed to hospital and again he nearly died. And he'd nearly died a few times. Javier, the boys and I went up to the hospital to see him. He was so small in his frame for sixteen. He grabbed onto you like he knew he was going to be going soon. He could hardly breathe. Alex was angelic with a mischievous side; he was always disappointed with the size of his frame and his height. He wanted to be tall and well-built, not small and frail. Maxine had forgotten he was allergic to Vegemite and had put it on his sandwiches, which caused his asthmatic reaction. Alex recovered and returned home from hospital and things were back to normal. Alex was small but tough. He liked to try to do all the things the other boys did, like play football. He went camping with his dad, and fishing; he rode his bikes, both motor and bicycle. He was in Little Athletics, and he played cricket. But as he got closer to his sixteenth birthday on the twelfth of April, his frailty showed more and more.

In May, 1987, in the late afternoon, I was in the lounge room with Javier and the boys. We were watching TV and the phone rang. I got up and answered it.

It was a distress call from Geoffrey, Alex's brother. 'Aunty Chris, come quickly, it's Alex, come – I think he's dying,' Geoffrey fearfully told me.

I became distressed. 'Oh, Geoffrey, no, where's your mum?' I asked.

He said, 'Up the street getting tea.'

My heart sank, and again, I said, 'Oh, Geoffrey,' and I started to cry. Then I froze. I heard his desperate calls for help: 'Aunty Chris, come.'

The reality hit me. 'Did you call an ambulance?'

He struggled and said, 'Yes.'

'I am coming,' I said, and with that I put the phone down and went to run out of the house, and Javier asked, 'Where are you going?'

'To Alex,' I answered.

He smirked, asking, 'Why?'

I looked at him with disgust, because he was sitting there and had heard the conversation, and said, 'He's dying.'

He looked at me and said, 'Wait here.'

I said, 'No, Javier, I won't wait here. You wouldn't let me go to Geoffrey and Alex last time when they were in trouble. But this time I am going.'

Javier was so angry with me. I hesitated for a second and then left the house. Outside, I felt pulled by my nephew Geoffrey and his distress, and I felt the distress I would have to face later on with Javier. But I would not abide by his rules for peace, when Alex and Geoffrey were in need of me. I would have to face Javier later on.

I was almost at Maxine's house. I didn't know what to expect or what I would find. Would I see Alex dead? I quickened my pace, running, and thought, Oh please no, not Alex. I had seen the anguish on Alex's face last time he suffered an asthma attack. He was so breathless. As I neared their property, I saw people in their yard. The ambulance men were there. They were taking Alex out on a stretcher. He had on a breathing apparatus. I stopped for a second and stared, thinking, *Where's*

Maxine? She will be devastated. I could see Geoffrey; he was so young. I walked closer. Everything seemed like it was in slow motion. Their neighbour, Janice, was consoling Geoffrey. But I could see he was numb from the experience.

Then he spotted me. 'Aunty Chris.'

'Oh, Geoff,' I responded, putting my arms around him, as we watched the ambulance people put Alex in the ambulance.

Geoffrey cried, 'I didn't know what to do, Aunty Chris.'

'You did the right thing, Geoffrey.'

The ambulance men pushed the stretcher into the vehicle. One of them got in the back with Alex; the other closed the back door, and as he did, Maxine pulled into their driveway. She jumped out of her car and screamed out, 'What's going on?'

'Mum, it's Alex,' Geoffrey said in a timid voice, still holding on to me.

'What happened to Alex?' she asked, not thinking the worst.

The ambulance man asked, 'Are you his mother?'

'Yes,' she snapped.

Geoffrey said, 'I think he's dying, Mum.'

Then the reality hit her. She became hysterical. The ambulance man tried to calm her down and told her to go with them to the hospital. He helped her into the back of the vehicle with the other ambulance man and Alex.

'Chris, you'll stay with Geoffrey?'

'Yes, of course I will,' I said as the door was closed on them. The other man rushed to the front of the vehicle, immediately started the ambulance with the siren going, and drove off in the direction of the hospital.

I stayed with Geoffrey, and he explained to me what had happened. 'Aunty Chris, I couldn't find the ventilator medicine.' I glanced at the machine on the floor. 'I called the ambulance,' he cried, 'but they didn't believe me.'

He really cried, and I cried with him. 'Geoffrey, why didn't you call me earlier? When you first noticed a problem,' I asked with softness and compassion, holding him in my arms.

'I didn't think to, Aunty Chris.'

I thought, *Of course, he's only a child.* Comfortingly, I said, 'It's okay, Geoffrey.'

He asked me, 'Do you think he will be all right?'

I half smiled, holding him, and said, 'Yes, Geoff, let's hope so.'

I listened to him as he explained how the ambulance people thought they were kids playing a joke. He looked at me and said, 'I told them I wasn't joking, my brother was dying.' His eyes were full of a lack of understanding as to why people wouldn't believe him.

'Oh, Geoffrey,' I cried as he told me, and my heart hurt for him. Then he told me he had to go and get the neighbour to ring the ambulance, then they came.

'Aunty Chris, I didn't know what to do for Alex,' he confessed. He stared at me for reassurance and an answer.

'Geoffrey, you did all you could do. You called the ambulance and you went next door – you did what you had to do.'

I listened as he told me how they were looking for the medicine for the vaporiser, and they both couldn't find it. I looked at Geoffrey and I felt for him, and thought, why? And as I pondered, I saw whose child was to be taken. *Why Alex kept echoing in my mind.* Geoff kept telling me over and over, and I just listened and reassured him that he did all he could do. My thoughts drifted to how he and Alex couldn't find the ventilator medicine, and when Alex couldn't find it, he must have known then and there he was going to die this time.

Geoffrey had settled. He'd stopped talking. I gently moved my arm from around him and said, 'I'd better call Uncle Javier.' His little face in its innocence, with tears still flowing from his little pink eyes, nodded yes. I rang Javier and as the number was being rung through, I dreaded hearing his voice and what he would say.

'Hello,' he said.

I explained to him what had happened, and I told him it was very serious, and that Alex had been rushed to hospital. I informed him I would stay with Geoffrey until one of his parents came home.

But of course, he was angry. I could hear it in the tone of his voice – it had a sarcastic ring to it. He told me to come home. I said, 'No, Javier, I am staying with Geoffrey until his father or Maxine come home, and Maxine asked me to stay. I told her I will.' And he hung up on me. For once, I didn't care what he thought or how much crap I'd have to face later on; I was staying.

Collin came home. He didn't know what had happened. I had to tell him and said as calmly and gently as I could, 'Collin, Alex has been rushed to hospital, he'd had an asthma attack and Maxine is with him.' He cried and turned away. His heart was immediately breaking. I felt that he sensed this time it was bad. He went to the lounge room and he sat and sobbed and sobbed. There was nothing I could do but be there for them both and sit and wait with them.

Geoffrey and I sat holding each other while Collin suffered in his own pain, and his pain was so great. He slowly came around, asking Geoffrey what had happened. The child said, 'Mum went up the street for dinner and we were playing, and Alex started to wheeze, he asked for his vaporiser. I got the vaporiser out, but I couldn't find the medicine for it. I looked and he got worse, so I called the ambulance and they didn't believe me. I ran to Janice and she rang them and got the ambulance here. I called Aunty Chris later.' Collin twisted in pain and threw his face into his hands. Geoffrey and I waited for him to gather himself. Both Geoffrey and I cried too. We were all distraught. Collin had already lost his sister, and now maybe his son. The house was cold and silent, and there was already emptiness about it, as if someone was missing. The only noises were those of our tears and pain and the hum of the fish tank. My eyes diverted to the tank to find solace in the water and the movement of the lone, large fish that swam endlessly back and forth in his small confined space of six feet, compared to the great expanse of his natural habitat.

We went to look for the medicine. But we couldn't find it. Collin broke down and wept again. He asked me if I would stay with Geoffrey. I said yes, with a nod to doubly confirm I'd stay, smiling only to reassure him not to worry, I'd look after Geoffrey. Geoffrey jumped in, telling his dad that he wanted to go with him to the hospital. Collin looked at Geoffrey and sadly said,

'Okay, come, it might be best.' So they went to the hospital.

I watched them drive off, then I began to walk home. As I walked, I wondered why Alex had to die. I already knew he was gone. I thought of their house; it too felt cold. Sadness seemed to envelope the house already, and it seemed to have lost its light – and Alex was their light.

Chapter 11

Death Helps Those Left Behind To Understand Life

I walked home slowly. I was already in hot water with Javier; a few more minutes up or down wouldn't matter. I arrived at our front gate; as I opened it, the click of the latch aroused Candy. She came running to greet me. I walked up the path with the dog, and she jumped around my feet. I patted her as we walked. We both rounded the corner of the house to the back door. I gave her an extra big pat and rubbed her ears, as I drew the courage that I needed from her. Taking a deep breath, I stepped up onto the patio, opened the back door with some trepidation, and walked into the kitchen, going straight into the lounge room where they were still watching TV.

Javier and the boys were laughing. 'Well, what happened?' he asked. I explained. I told Javier that this time it was very serious, and that I didn't think Alex would live. But Javier didn't believe me. I think they thought it was just another asthma attack and Alex would recover. Javier and the boys kept chatting amongst themselves. Javier wasn't really talking to me because I'd gone up to Alex.

I waited for news about Alex and the phone rang. I answered it. It was my dad, and he broke the news to me, saying, 'Alex's died, Chrissy.'

'Oh, Dad, no, he didn't,' I cried.

'He died, Chrissy.'

I said to Dad, 'I'll come to the hospital to be with Maxine.'

He said, 'No, they're in a bad way and they'll go home soon, and Mum and I will go with them.'

'Okay, Dad, I'll call you later on.' Dad hung up and I placed the phone receiver down. Tears were rolling down my face.

I felt numb as I cried. I turned and said, 'Alex died.'

Julian immediately broke down. 'Mum, he didn't?'

'Yes, Julian, he died.' Julian dropped his face into his hands and then looked up at his father; he had gone serious. I think Julian really wanted to come with me to see Alex, but his father would have held him back. I understood he couldn't go against his father. The pain was so great for me and Julian, losing Alex, and for me it was like losing one of my own children.

I had to bear this thought in silence. Because if I showed too much concern over Alex, it would be the worst thing I could do in that moment. After that day, I really lost all respect for Javier; I had none at all. Julian went off to his room and cried. I went in and talked to him. Jerod was upset too, but not to the extent that Julian was.

That night was quiet. No one uttered a word. I rang Dad, but no one answered. I didn't want to call Maxine. Later on, I called Dad again and he answered the phone. I asked if they wanted me to go over, and again, Dad said no, they were too distressed and to go tomorrow.

In bed that night, I cried inwardly in silence and asked, 'Why, why did Alex have to die?' I knew death was part of life, that we were born and died. I knew some had to die earlier to help the living deal with death and loss of loved ones. Maxine was the one to lose her child, and she'd been prepared for this moment all those years ago by attending the funerals of Grandma's family or friends. Maxine was the one to bear witness to Grandma's grief and loneliness. But I think I was the one to feel her grief. As I lay there, my bed felt cold. I couldn't talk to Javier about Alex. I softly sobbed all night, and I had to bear the pain of losing Alex, for his parents, but mostly for Geoffrey. He was just a child, and he'd have to face the guilt of not being able to help Alex. In my restlessness I asked, 'Why?' I had to question it.

The next day, we went up to Maxine's house. It felt strange facing my sister. I asked myself over and over, Why? My real feelings went out to Collin. I felt for him the most, because I knew the grief he had to face for the rest of his life. Collin was a very deep and sensitive man; to lose Alex not long after his sister just added to his grief. He had experienced the loss of his sister and his son. My grandma had experienced the loss of her husband and her son. Life is a cycle, and we can follow similar paths to those gone before us or those in our lives. What are we carrying in our memories? How is it we follow the same things other people experience or do? How was it that I was getting these messages that someone was going to die? I wouldn't understand the deeper reality of all of this until many, many years had passed by.

I felt for Maxine, but I knew she'd recover, because she was emotionally stronger than Collin. Geoffrey was silent when I entered the house. He looked up at me. I could see he blamed himself. He was only a child and he'd done his best. The flower tributes poured in. This hit home the reality of the situation. Maxine was devastated. Collin cried. Collin was a man's man who never cried in public. That day his vulnerability was exposed. It was hard to know what to say. Maxine asked me, 'Chris, why?' I couldn't answer her. I didn't have any answers that she would've understood. It wasn't the time to tell her that life comes and life goes, and some choose to leave early to help the ones they leave behind.

In their house it was so cold and vacant, and I asked myself, 'Am I right in my thinking, and is it the truth?' Looking at them, I thought about how I'd feel if this death was my child. I looked at them in their grief and asked myself, what can I do? There was nothing I could do but be there for them.

That day there was a viewing of Alex's body to say goodbye to him. I wanted to go and say my goodbyes, but Maxine wouldn't let me or any of us go and see Alex. Only she, Geoffrey and Collin went. I was devastated and torn with her decision. I wanted so much to see Alex. Javier and I went to the hospital with them, but we waited for them while they went in to say farewell to Alex. While waiting, I told Javier how I really wanted to go and see Alex. He coolly reminded me, 'Well, you can't, she doesn't want you to.' I had to inwardly bear this hurt. Javier was so bitter, and all I wanted to do was say my farewells to Alex. I loved both

Alex and Geoffrey as my own children, even though I could never confess that to Javier.

I looked over at Javier's surly face and thought of how I could never tell my sister's boys that I loved them in front of him. I did it once, when my boys were younger. I couldn't help myself; my love just welled up inside of me. I had to express that love to my nephews.

Every now and then I'd get those intense feelings of love, which overwhelmed me. My feelings of love were so strong for those around me, I'd just have to express them to those I loved. Many times, this happened when Javier wasn't around, and I could freely hug and say 'I love you.' Other times I'd forget myself and say it in his presence. I'd cuddle Maxine's boys and kiss them. When Alex and Geoffrey left the house, Javier turned on me and announced to our boys, 'See, your mother loves your cousins more than you pair, did you see her cuddling and kissing them?'

I stared at him in surprise and shock. Did he hate my family that much? I shook my head, stating, to protect my boys, 'That's not true, Javier, and you know that. You too must love your sister's children, nearly as much as your own children.' But I knew he didn't love them, at all. Javier was even prejudiced against his own family, and if you didn't have a certain look, or you didn't look right in his eyes, he didn't like you, regardless of you being family or not.

My boys didn't react in these situations. I guessed they couldn't. They just looked at both of their parents and stayed out of the whole situation.

Any other time I would not have been able to control myself, and I would have screamed at him and gone off. This time I didn't, because deep down something told me if I did react to this situation, maybe my boys would have thought I did love their cousins more than them. I was walking on eggshells to protect myself and my boys, and I didn't want to prove their father right. Javier was always one step ahead of me. He could be a cruel person in these situations. I hated him more and more. I couldn't wait for the day when I could leave him.

Now he didn't have to worry about Alex gaining any love from me. Alex's death left us all with emptiness in our lives. Especially for Julian, because I knew he loved his cousin so much. I remember when Julian was about eight, Alex had gone off with his friend Sam, leaving Julian. Julian was devastated. He rushed home and told me that Alex didn't love him because he went off and played with Sam. I had to explain to him that it wasn't because he didn't love him; it was just that they were friends, and sometimes friends needed to play separately, without cousins. I reassured him that later on Alex would come and play with him, too.

Nonetheless, Alex's death wasn't an easy time for any of us. Death wasn't talked about in our house. Sometimes I wished I'd spoken about life and death to my boys. Not that I had the answers back then. I was pretty ignorant about life and death myself. The ideas I did have around life and death wouldn't go down well with Javier, anyway. The idea that we all will die, and it is part of the cycle of life, and those who choose to go first are doing so to help others in their family or friendship circles to learn something they need to learn. I knew with life came death. At that time, I didn't understand why I was getting these warnings around the death of people near to me. Where was that coming from? I had no answers, I just got the feelings. I couldn't tell Javier I was getting these feelings that there was going to be a death. That would only have given him more fuel to poke fun at me with the boys. So I kept my thoughts and my feelings to myself.

Chapter 12

The Funeral – But More Death Surrounds Us

Alex's funeral was very big. Maxine wanted me to be with her. So in public, Javier had to let me go and be with her. If he objected, I was still going to go with her, because she needed my support. All Alex's school friends came to the funeral. I don't think I'd seen so many people at a funeral in this town. The sadness was overwhelming for Maxine, Collin and Geoffrey. As I looked around, I felt that this wasn't the end and Alex wasn't in that box. I knew life went on and I even felt his presence there watching us. I found comfort in knowing he was still with us. After the funeral, they only had family go to the house, and it was so trying for all of us. All we could do was be there for them. Maxine took time off work, but she could only stay at home for a week and had to go back to work. She said she couldn't stay in the house and needed to get out because too many people were coming to the house; she found this bothered her. Collin struggled more than Maxine, and he continued to struggle for many years. They had lots of counselling over that year to come to terms with the death of Alex.

Geoffrey told us that the night of his brother's death, Alex had come to him and sat on his bed and told Geoffrey that he was all right and not to worry. Maxine could not understand why Alex went to Geoffrey and not her, and in my innocence, I said, without really realising, 'They go to the ones who can handle it the best.' She knew I was right.

Maxine was scared of being in the house alone. She couldn't handle being alone there, right up until she left the house. Sometimes she'd take their blue cattle dog into the house to keep her company. Collin continued to go camping and shooting; I think the solitude of the bush comforted him, allowing him to cry. Being a sensitive person, his sadness was so great. I think the bush allowed him that privacy to lay bare his emotions. Nature is the best place for a sensitive person. Collin wore a tough outer shell and that shell was only a disguise for his true self. Maxine would never admit this about him. They were very individual in their marriage. Sometimes I longed for that individuality for my own marriage. I felt couples should be able to express themselves individually. If Javier had been more open to allowing me to express myself and go for the goals I wanted, our marriage may have survived.

All Maxine and Collin's married life, they were doing their own things. That had to be about trust. Collin was the complete opposite to Javier; he never encroached on Maxine's freedom, and she in turn never encroached on his freedom. However, Alex's death separated them until they grew apart.

Alex's death was followed by other family members' deaths, all happening one after the other in the same week, and it was unbelievable. First, we got news from Queensland that my cousin Naomi's daughter Becky Anne, who was six, was killed on the road. The same week we got news about my Aunty Kay's son Sammy dying from an asthma attack, aged twenty-six. Years later we found out that my long-lost cousin Henry died around the same time from a heart attack, aged thirty-six.

Alex was sixteen years old. So many losses in that week. All with the digit six in their ages. And they all were born in a year ending with a one.

I was told my Uncle Donny was seventeen when he died. But I found out from Dad that he was eighteen when he'd died in 1936. He was my grandma's first child. There had to be a link to all of this. So far, I didn't understand it, and I didn't understand what was happening in our family.

My Aunty Kay had two families: her first husband was Pete and they had four children. Aunty Kay left Uncle Pete years ago. Sammy was one of their four children. After their separation, Sammy and his two brothers, Lance and Brandon, and their sister Leigh, went to live with their grandma on Uncle Pete's side. All these children from that marriage did very well for themselves. Lance became a teacher, Leigh became a nurse, and Brandon served in the Air Force. I felt these four children were lucky to go and live with their grandma, because they all got a better chance in life. Unfortunately, Sammy died to leave a hole in their lives. And my aunty's second marriage, to a man called Rex, produced four more children who didn't fare as well.

We always thought Aunty Betty had six children. There was so much unrest in our families where marriage was concerned, and many surprises. Henry was a surprise to us all; we didn't know about him at all and nor did my aunty's six other children. Anyway, Henry showed up after many years and made himself known to the family, even attending my wedding. But Henry came and Henry went just as fast. We never, ever saw him again. I wasn't sure if any of my aunty's children ever saw him again, either. Henry had the same dad as Kelvin. We thought Kelvin was our eldest cousin to Aunty Betty, but it was Henry who was the oldest.

Aunty Betty had done what her mother, Grandma Henderson, whom I always knew as Grandma Owens, had done.

My Aunty Betty left her marriage, taking only one child with her and leaving the other children behind. Mum told me that Aunty Betty had a tragic life as a teenager and she really loved a very special man called Jerry when she was eighteen. But Grandma forbid her from seeing Jerry, and after that Aunty Betty went wild and rebelled against Grandma, causing herself a lot of pain and a mixed-up life. I really loved my Aunty Betty – she was my second-favourite aunty. There were so many secrets in my mum's family. It all intrigued me.

Chapter 13

Giving My Children Quality Experiences

When I married, I only wanted to have boys and no girls. I loved my boys so much and I didn't want them to have the same type of life that I'd had as a child. When I found out I was pregnant with Julian, I listed all the activities he'd be doing to make sure he had the full benefit of a good childhood, and on that list was university. All my children that I'd have would be attending university, and they all were going to play all kinds of sport and join different clubs for kids; and they did. I was determined to break the family cycle of non-achievers and no university-trained adults, and as far as I was concerned, young people needed to be in group activities to develop their social skills. The only achiever in our family was Uncle Donny. Before his death he'd achieved so much and even won a place in the 1936 Olympics, which he never got to because he died that same year. He had scrolls and awards from his school, and he was an all-rounder in the field of sport.

My plan came to fruition, and as time moved on, I realised many things one must do when one has children. I was especially protective of and wary of the 'bogeyman' concept. My father delighted in scaring us as children and I didn't want these scary beliefs put on my boys. Children can develop lots of fears around the unknown through the ignorance of others. For me, though, the most important thing was to give my children their freedom. There was one other requirement: if they joined a sport or an activity, they had to give it at least one year's trial before they quit, and both the boys agreed to this. It was a good form of discipline and honouring of the self to a commitment. They had many opportunities, especially in sport.

They both played cricket, joined Little Athletics, did swimming and football, and Julian even joined the Cubs for a year. Julian played the classical guitar and stuck with his music, even though he hated to practise. Even though it wasn't his love, he excelled in his music, much to his instructor Timothy's amazement. When I told Timothy Julian didn't practise much, he was amazed because Julian was playing complex classical tunes. Julian was gifted, but didn't realise how gifted he was. Or he didn't want to realise it. At that stage of my life, I too didn't understand how gifted he was and how to nurture those gifts. Not being musical, and restricted in my own married life, I had issues around putting myself forward. How could I help him when I couldn't help myself? He ended up taking up Spanish Flamenco music and he was excellent at it.

Both boys eventually gave up football for Taekwondo, and I was so pleased. But they both played football for their school teams at St Benedict's, and a couple of years later they both re-joined their local district football club in Hastings Crossing. Both of them did really well with Taekwondo. However, Julian was an all-rounder and excelled in football, and he won a position in his school team to play in the prestigious football events. St Benedict's kept winning and got to the grand final and were on TV playing. From that game, Julian was spotted by talent scouts and offered a position in a Rosemont team to play for Waynedale Club. But that meant we would have had to move from Hastings Crossing to Rosemont, and we decided not to. Julian wasn't too keen about moving and leaving his friends at that stage of his life. We gave him a choice in the decision. He chose to stay where we were.

I wanted my boys to experience a different world from mine. They got those opportunities and they succeeded in whatever they experienced, as well as having a lot of support and encouragement. As a mum I offered my help as much as I could give them in all areas of their lives. Most importantly, I listened to them and above all, I loved them.

In my marriage – my 'sleeping years', I call them – there was one thing I neglected to do, and that was to confide in my boys about my spiritual beliefs. If I had, I may have opened them up on their paths in that area. However, both my boys are very closed in regard to spirituality. They have no tolerance or understanding of me in regard to my spirituality. I made lots of mistakes in my marriage. I felt I neglected to teach the boys about love and compassion. But how could I, when I was in so much grief, and possibly depression, myself. I was questioning life, and in my own isolation I was seeking answers to the meaning of all around me. Solace in my own world helped me to understand life by observing it through others. I had no idea who I was and where I'd come from and what I had to do. Where I was in this marriage, there was no way for me to go to school, to take courses to understand what was being brought up in me, so my questions would have to wait to be answered in later life. Inside me, I knew things without knowing; I couldn't help my boys without first helping myself. How could I help them without knowing myself? For now, I was providing the basics of life. To live in a mundane life. Someone had forgotten to tell me why I was here, so I lived totally in the physical world and emotional world, bordering onto the spiritual world in secret and in fear of the unknown.

I loved my two boys way too much and I would tell them when they were little that they were the most beautiful boys in the world. And we parents need to really think about what we say to our children, because it can have a devastating effect on them or wound them forever. For what we say and think about our own children isn't always true in their experiences with other people, as they journey with these other people. Because what I thought of my boys was not necessarily true for others. The role of a parent is a big responsibility, and we aren't taught how to care for something as precious as a child. We have to get a licence to drive a car, by having a test for competency, but there are no tests to be a parent.

I wanted my boys to develop their own assessment of life and not take on the beliefs of others, not even my own beliefs; even though I feel we all need guidance, and from the guidance we should let the child make up their own conclusions. Our beliefs should come from within us. As a child I got information no one told me about. So are we getting information within us? Are children receiving their own information? If so, how can we question what a child sees as not true? Nonetheless, this is what happens if it doesn't fit into our family's pattern of thought: it's squashed. Who gives the family or others in the family circle the right to ridicule the children or adults in the group for their thoughts? Children should be respected for their thoughts and feelings.

In 1988 Jerod went to Bali with St Benedict's High School. He went with Mr Long, his Asian Studies teacher – the same teacher Julian had. Jerod and Julian actually seemed to do very similar things throughout their lives. Jerod also broke his front tooth, but he did this before he even left Australia. They must have been copying each other. Jerod's incident happened late in the afternoon on the day before he was to fly out to Indonesia. He was mucking around with some friends; a stone was thrown in a joke and the stone hit Jerod's front tooth. This threw us into a small chaos trying to get a dentist to do an after-hours job. But we managed to find one and his tooth was fixed.

I had to stop work in April 1988 at the egg-collecting farms. It had been good and helped us with a better quality of life. Nonetheless, it was time to put an end to this job. I was so glad to stop working there. However, it meant I was at home with Javier every day, and that wasn't easy. I'd worked at the farms for seven and a half years and felt I'd served some kind of penance there. It was hard, dirty, manual work. I lost a lot of myself there as I had to comply with others or be ostracised. All I wanted was to fit in and be accepted. The hardest thing was being laughed at for my intelligence because I was using words unfamiliar to those I worked with. Again, the same old story: I had to change my behaviours to suit others, instead of standing steadfast and saying no and remaining myself. I found I was not a strong personality, and it wasn't easy to be different and be accepted by the majority. Sometimes it was too difficult for me to cope with. If you're different and don't comply with the majority in a group, I found you're soon shunned. I had no friends of my own at home and I needed some company outside of my family group. However, my workmates weren't the company I was longing for.

I used to try to bring my thoughts into their world gradually, but they had no inclination towards spirituality. They never thought about the wonders of the world, or the greater meaning behind why things happened in the world or in the family. I was curious about the origin of man. They never wondered about the world and how it worked or anything interesting in their families' history. Daily living was all they were interested in. So I wasn't sad to see the end of that place – there, I wasn't feeding my brain the right food. I'd read all the books I had and soon had nothing new to read. I couldn't get any new books so again I limited myself in knowledge. I had to go back to the old ways, just keeping house and living daily. My speech deteriorated more and more. I was ridiculed by my boys and Javier, and I couldn't get out of the situation. I had to just hold on. It would be another three years before we could move out of Hastings Crossing.

This was to be Julian's last year at high school, then to university and the start of a better life. I was so pleased my sons were happy to go to university. They could see the trials one faced without an education.

At the end of this last year in high school he let me know he would never play the guitar again. It was his choice, but I did tell him he would regret it. So the guitar was stored away with a broken string.

Julian had no set ideas of what he wanted to study at university, but it all fell into his lap. Initially, he wanted to be a detective in the Federal Police, but he was unable to because he was colour blind. He also would have liked to join the Armed Forces, but again his being colour blind prevented him from any military career. His other choice was a physical education teacher, but oddly enough you have to have very high scores to get into that course. The same for sports medicine, which was an option in career choices: unfortunately, his mark wasn't high enough. He ended up scanning the newspapers for ideas and saw endless job opportunities in nursing. It was a university entry career and the jobs available made it a secure job – there was an abundance of positions for nurses. So Julian chose nursing as a career, and reasoned that he'd have a secure job for life. We were very lucky because the government had brought in fee exemption for nursing courses up until 1993, due to there being a shortage of nurses.

So Julian applied to do nursing at the university in Dawson Hill and his path was laid out for him in the health industry. I was happy for him and my job as a mother was fulfilled.

He continued playing football and Taekwondo.

Chapter 14

Intuition About Death
And Finding Out About
Family Habits

It was 1989; Julian was at university and he was managing driving to Dawson Hill. I woke not feeling my normal self and felt edgy; I had that feeling again, the one I got when there was something about to happen.

I said to Javier, 'Javier, I feel like something is going to happen to us and I feel like it's a death, and we don't have a will made up for the boys.'

He looked at me strangely and informed me, 'You're mad.' This was his favourite saying to me when he couldn't understand me or didn't want to understand my world; to him, I was always mad or stupid.

The morning continued and the boys had gone off to school. The restless feeling got more intense and my body was getting more and more upset.

'Javier, I'm really worried about us going to Rosemont, and we don't have a will for the boys. The feeling is getting stronger,' I declared. He stared at me. I could see he was losing his patience. It was too early for us to make our way to Rosemont. By the look on his face I realised I had gone too far. So I remained quiet, and I couldn't say any more on the subject or he would be really upset with me. We had a big day ahead of us travelling to Rosemont, and I wanted some peace of mind and a smooth trip.

Rosemont was about a three-hour drive away. That day I was so nervous. We were collecting the papers we needed before we left the house and the phone rang. I looked at Javier, because he was in two minds about whether to answer it or not. I felt he should answer it. He did.

'Hello.' He was talking to the caller in a mild voice, because I think I had unnerved him by then. I heard, 'Oh, Max, how are you, mate?' I realised it was my dad. Javier relaxed and his whole persona and tone changed. As I waited, Javier said, 'I am sorry, Max, I will put your daughter on.' Javier handed me the phone, not saying a word but looking glum.

I asked, 'Yes, Dad, what is it?' Dad told me why he'd called us. As I listened to him, my whole body changed and relaxed; the feeling of impending death left me. Dad told me Uncle Mitch had died. I told Dad I had this feeling all morning that there was going to be a death. But Dad was like Javier: he couldn't understand such feelings. Then, I knew who had died. It wasn't to be us to face death, it was my Uncle Mitch. Dad and I talked for a short period. I gave him my condolences and asked him about my cousins, Gerry, Hope, and Charlene, but he hadn't heard from them yet. Sonia, Uncle Mitch's partner, had informed him. I told Dad I'd get back to him because we had to go to Rosemont.

So we went to Rosemont with me feeling much better. Actually, relieved knowing who had died. As we travelled silently together, I thought, *Why is it I get these feelings and no one else in my family does?* All I could do was ponder over the morning's happenings. I needed to speak to Javier. So I started up a conversation on Mitch's parting and his only comment was, 'Well, he's had a good innings.' Well, so much for understanding. Again I was left questioning in my mind about life.

That wasn't good enough, and I said, 'But he hadn't had a good innings. He's only in his sixties, he was sixty-six.' Looking over towards Javier, I thought, *I can't show too much concern with Uncle's death; he'll get annoyed I am thinking of other people.* I thought of my cousins and wondered how they were feeling. The less said the better.

On talking to Hope, Uncle Mitch's youngest daughter – who was the most affected by her father's death, because deep down I think she was the only one that had any love for him – Hope told me that he hadn't left a will. He had told her that he hadn't made up a will yet. It hit me why I was so frantic about Javier and I not having a will. Maybe I had been picking up on my Uncle Mitch's last concerns before his death?

However, there was a written will that was later found in the boot of his car. This will stated that Sonia, the woman he was living with, got everything he owned. Another strange event in our family history, and again history was repeating itself, with my Uncle Mitch doing what his mother did to him and Dad, by leaving everything to his sister Connie. And the property Grandma gave to Connie will probably be passed onto her husband Oliver, an outsider of the family. Why is it in this family that outsiders will get the possessions that are meant to go to family members? Again, it had happened, Uncle Mitch had given his possessions to a partner and not his own daughters. He did what his mother did to him. He cursed his sister Connie and Grandma, then did it himself. Is there a force within us that sets a path we must follow?

Hope was adamant that her father had told her he had changed his mind and that he was going to change his will. Unfortunately, he must not have gotten around to doing that before he died. His death was sudden and unexpected; a heart attack. Dad and Connie also had heart issues.

Uncle Mitch had virtually ended up living a pauper's life, like Connie was with Oliver. He was living in a caravan down the back of this woman Sonia's property. Sonia treated him like dirt, and we all wondered why he took all the crap she dished out on him. He'd never let his wife Kimberly get away with that. Often Sonia humiliated him in front of everyone, calling him a mouse, which he became: a mouse who feared her. He'd given Kimberly and other women a lot of abuse in his earlier days, and then he accepted abuse from Sonia. He'd mellowed in his later years, we all reasoned.

Uncle Mitch had condemned Grandma for giving everything to Connie. He was furious, more so than my dad. Grandma had left all her money and the house at Sandy Lake to Connie. This caused so much bitterness between Connie, Mitch, and Dad. As time went on, my dad forgave his sister, but Uncle Mitch never forgave her. Then he went and did the same thing to his own daughters. My question was, why? Why are we so propelled to act in a certain way? It was hard for his own daughters to comprehend as well, seeing how he had condemned his sister.

Again, the immediate family lost money or property to questionable spouses or partners. We had this failing in our family where money or property was given to outsiders and the family lost out. And those who gave it away came close to living in poverty, due to their spouse or partner ruling their lives. In Connie's case, the man she'd drawn in was living in poverty and he pulled her down to his level. Ask why and you'd soon find out.

Many years later in my own life, I would experience this phenomenon and nearly come close to poverty myself.

Money does weird things to families. My cousins lost their inheritance, as did my father and Uncle Mitch. It was also weird because my favourite aunt had turned on me, too, when Grandma had died; she told my father she wanted him to get the money I had borrowed from Grandma for my first car. When Dad told me Aunty Connie wanted that money back, I looked at him, thinking, *How will I pay that back?* Dad must have seen the look on my face and told me not to worry about it. He was pleased someone got something out of Grandma's estate. It all went over my head and I never gave it another thought, because really, Dad had arranged for me to borrow that money from Grandma; I didn't personally ask her for it.

Nonetheless, there were a lot of issues around our family when it came to death. For me, death wasn't the end, and the material gains people made have never impressed me to want to fight for them.

Chapter 15

Changing The Family Dynamics

In December 1989, Javier's case was won and completed. Life was changing. I talked Javier into moving to Dawson Hill to live. I was ready to move. So was Julian; he wanted to leave Hastings Crossing as well. This was our chance. On the weekends, Julian and I went house-hunting. We wanted to find a house in Dawson Hill now that he was at university.

Both the boys were still playing football: Julian was now playing for the local Hastings Crossing football team in the first-grade division, and Jerod was playing for his school and the local juniors' team in Hastings Crossing. Unfortunately, Jerod developed a stress fracture in his spine, so he was unable to play football anymore, which was disheartening for him. He tried a couple of times because he loved the sport, but after ten minutes, he was off the field. We took him to the best doctor in our district, Dr Edwards, and he referred us to a Rosemont doctor for further analysis. Jerod was offered an operation to place a rod in his back, but he declined, and the decision was his at the age of sixteen, Jerod was given the right to decide for himself as an adult. They had to make their own decisions regarding their own bodies. We did discuss it as a family and weighed up all the pros and cons from the doctor's advice, but Jerod had the last say. He went back to doing Taekwondo and worked for his black belt.

At this time, Julian had obtained his black belt in Taekwondo and was given an instructor's job out at Spencer Shire Community Centre; there he met Gerry, and they fell madly in love. Gerry was also attending Dawson Hill University doing nursing, but she was a year ahead of Julian because she was five months older than him. Now this was happening, I told Javier it was time for the boys to bring home their girlfriends, now that they were older and more sexually active, because I didn't want them going off to parks or getting into any awkward situations, and preferred them to be in the safety of their own home; and if they wanted to be sexually active, then they could be in their own beds. Javier agreed to this; after all, they were adults. I wanted to respect them in their adulthood.

So we allowed them to have their girlfriends at home, to experience their changes in the comfort of their own home. It was discussed with the boys and they were happy about this decision, so they started to have their girlfriends stay over, with the permission of the girl's family, of course. But Jerod hadn't brought home his girlfriend, Emily, to stay with us in our Hastings Crossing house; he'd go and stay over at her house. It was just Julian who had brought home Gerry first.

Chapter 16

Mum's Fears Play Out In My Brother's Life

Tragedy hit home, and all my mum's fears about Dad leaving her came to play out in her beloved son's life. Lorna announced after New Year's Day that she was leaving Barton. She had been his wife for sixteen years, and she walked out of his life with Barton's best friend Michael, who happened to be related to Dianne, one of the girls in my primary school that I overheard talking about her sexual encounters with her father. Michael was supposed to have been happily married to Timothy and Penny's sister, Jessica.

When I heard the news about Lorna leaving Barton, I was so shocked, because all these people had some bearing on my own life from childhood, when I was caught in the shed with Timothy by Penny and my sister Maxine, and Maxine ran off and told my grandma what I was doing and caused me lots of pain and humiliation. I was already facing sexual abuse from Dad back then. Wow, it's such a small world, I thought, and all those memories came flooding back in. When I heard about Michael announcing he was going to leave Jessica, I remembered how embarrassed I was by that girl Penny at the age of ten. All these characters in the play of my life so far were resurfacing. Why was this happening? In my marriage, the memory of the sexual abuse from Dad popped up occasionally, and I'd seal it away in the back of my mind. *So why is the past resurfacing?* I thought.

Lorna left Barton and went with Michael. No one could believe it, and no one knew they were secretly having an affair. Barton wanted to kill them both, but Dad talked him out of that silly idea. Surprisingly, Dad actually helped Barton through this dark period of his life, supporting him. It was the first time I'd ever seen my father take an interest in Barton. I reasoned that Dad had had a similar experience when Mum left us all and went off with Alf Rush, which was so unexpected to all of us. Dad knew the pain a man felt when a woman he loved left him for another man.

Funny how the past comes and bites us on the bottom, so to say. And all those years Mum feared Dad walking away from her and going with Hilary. Was it her guilt for leaving Dad, and she thought he'd do payback on her and leave her for Hilary? But Mum really need not had feared that, because Dad wouldn't leave the farm for anyone, because that was his security and Hilary wasn't like mum's nature. No way would she be looking after Grandma. But if they were having a fling, it was causing Mum lots of pain and anguish just thinking it.

I didn't know what that feeling was like. To my knowledge, Javier never cheated on me. Although I had some suspicions with Nancy, Morton's wife, when he worked at Harper's Foundry. Also, on the cruise we went on in 1984–85, I felt he could have been involved with a couple of women. But truly, I didn't care anyway if he was. I never cheated on him, even though I did like some men from a distance. Funny, though, after all these years, everything was manifesting into Barton's reality.

Lorna left him with their three children, Hank, Dominic, and Sarah. Dominic was already having psychological problems and this incident pushed him even further into his own mayhem. It seemed to hit him the most at the age of thirteen. I had little to do with Barton's children, but Mum kept me informed about what was going on. I felt Dominic desperately needed his mother's affection. Lorna seem to lack that motherly affection for her kids at that stage of her life. I had seen her lash out verbally at them, when I felt they were trying to get her affection. But we never know the pain people feel, and I too had lashed out verbally in my dark days, towards my own boys. How the patterns run high in my family; I too wanted love and affection from my mother and never got it. I could understand how Dominic felt. The other two children, who were eleven and fourteen, seemed to brush off their mother's behaviour and stuck with their father. Grandma Henderson had left a family too, and we found that out after her death. She had four children to a previous marriage. She too must have deserted them. Lorna was following a pattern and disowning her family. Barton was the closest to Grandma Henderson – did he have the closest issues to work through with his grandma? At this stage of my life, I didn't have any clue as to what was happening in front of my eyes. But time would open my eyes and deeper understanding of family patterns would be revealed.

It was a hard time for Barton. He had the task of raising their three children on his own. Barton couldn't get over Lorna leaving him, causing him to constantly pine for her. It was so hard, because she was living in the same town – Hastings Crossing – as he was, and he could always run into her and Michael. Still, he wouldn't let her go. To me, it seemed worse than losing her to death; it would have been better to lose her in death than this way. Barton was feeling the pains of two grandmas. Did Grandma Henderson feel any pain leaving her first family? Grandma Kinread did feel the pain of her losses of her husband and son. That was obvious. She pined 'til she died. Maybe, though, she didn't quite do that to her own death, because I think she had dementia before she died. However, in her sanity, Grandma never resolved Grandfather leaving her, although it was through death. I guess my other grandma, Grandma Henderson, never resolved leaving her children to her first marriage.

It would take Barton about five years before he would look at another woman, because he would continue to live in hope that Lorna would return to him one day. Unfortunately, she never did return, and she had told Barton over and over to get on with his life. Nonetheless, time heals wounds for some. After about seven years they would become friends and heal the rift between them. Gradually, with time, he'd started to allow other women into his life, but once he did, he would experience many failed relationships. Somehow, I felt very close to my brother, not that we were ever close; to me he was like a stranger because of our separation in childhood, when Mum took him with her when she left Dad. And as a teenager Barton was away in a boy's home for a while. But on a larger scale, he and I had the biggest connection, though neither of us knew why. I felt we both didn't realise how affected we were by our past.

Chapter 17

Life Is Changing For All Of Us

At university, Julian started to meet some really nice friends who were also doing nursing. He was starting to bring them home and I seemed to get on really well with them. I overheard his friend Mitchell say, 'I wish your mum was my mum, she's so easy to talk to and live with.' I laughed to myself, thinking, *They're only seeing half the picture; they haven't glimpsed the devil locked up inside of me yet,* which I knew Javier and the boys had seen a few times. We never let anyone see the full story about our lives. We were always guarded, maybe unconsciously, and we all wore masks. My life back then had many masks.

It was March 1990, and Julian and I found the perfect house for us, and we couldn't wait to tell Javier. He was at work; he'd been put on light duties in a construction firm in Dawson Hill. He was back where he started in construction. It was good for him, and for me because he was back at work. When he came home that night, we told him we'd found the house we really liked. Julian and I were so excited, we could hardly contain ourselves. That weekend we went down to

Dawson Hill to look over the house with him; while in the house, Julian and I were pushing Javier into agreeing to buy it. We won him over. I think Julian was like me – he'd had enough of Hastings Crossing. We ended up buying the house. So now we'd be living in the suburb of Havertown, which I didn't particularly like. I don't know why I didn't like it, because Havertown was very nice and only ten minutes away from Claire Point Beach, which meant I was also going back in time to a place I used to frequent in my youth.

We put our house in Hastings Crossing on the market and it was snapped up in a few days. The new owner was the daughter of a school friend from Fenton Primary School, Annabel; she wasn't a close friend but a friend nonetheless. She and her daughter, Jane, were both ecstatic about our home and amazed at how well looked after it was. So now we only had to wait for the six-week transfer procedures and signing of contracts. Then we were off and out of Hastings Crossing.

Jerod was still in his last year of high school at St Benedict's in Wentworth, which was about thirty kilometres from Havertown. This wasn't an issue, because at sixteen, Jerod got his first car. He could drive himself to school from Dawson Hill to complete his last year, Year 12. Neither he nor we wanted him to start a new school in Dawson Hill for his last year. It was a bit of an inconvenience for Jerod. Nonetheless, he was okay about it.

On 28th April, 1990, we moved to Dawson Hill, away from Hastings Crossing. The new life in Dawson Hill didn't go down too well for the boys. Jerod and Julian were out in town and got into a fight and Jerod ended up breaking his leg. The break was so bad he had to get a pin put in the leg to support the break. We were fortunate and found a good doctor: Javier's doctor, Dr Harvey. He successfully operated on Jerod's leg. But the incident caused us all a lot of worries, because Jerod now had to get to school after he recuperated from the operation. Luckily, his car was an automatic, so he could drive it using his right leg.

So I had put everyone into a big spin moving, and into lots of changes. However, the boys were very resourceful, and I think that was because of my insistence that they take responsibility for their lives from age sixteen on and make a lot of their own decisions. The changes weren't too bad; they were more of an inconvenience, and each of us experienced some form of change. Nonetheless, and regardless of the initial upsets and mishaps that weren't too drastic, we all settled into our new home and city. I knew on a deeper level I had to get out of Hastings Crossing, or I would die there like my parents would. Mum always told me I would never leave Hastings Crossing and I would die there. Well, that wasn't for me, and it was time to escape my mother. Mum had still been putting her demands on me to work out her life, and she'd ring me up crying and complaining to me about Dad. She complained about how terribly he treated her. I'd suggest that she leave him, but she never would. So I copped her complaints and sometimes she'd hang up on me and put me into a bigger dilemma with her. I couldn't understand why she'd hang up on me. Then I'd be ringing her back up, or if I had the car, I'd go over to her when I was in Hastings Crossing. Now it was time for someone else to deal with Mum.

Jerod and Emily were still going out together, and she was now coming to stay with us, seeing as we were in Dawson Hill. Julian was now in his second year at university, and I had achieved my dream for my children that they were going to be university-educated.

Julian and Gerry were inseparable – they always seemed to be wrapped in each other's arms and entwined like snakes. They'd lie around the house constantly cuddling and kissing each other, much to Javier's disgust. He was always embarrassed by their actions. I don't think he approved. But they were in love, and I'd say, 'Let them be.'

My days in my marriage seemed to be getting longer. Javier was becoming a stranger to me. We didn't have anything in common. Even our conversation had stopped. Often, we were left to ourselves because the boys were busy with their lives, spending a lot of time away from home. Things were changing, especially for me. However, I felt nothing for Javier. He seemed to be the only one not experiencing any changes. He was still slotted in the 1960s. I started to open up and I felt big changes. These changes were coming in fast through my dreams. I wasn't aware at that time of my spiritual life. But my mind was. Also, I was opening up to new points of view of the world. All was being altered in my world.

I had amazing dreams of dinosaurs chasing me in a prehistoric jungle. They were chasing me out of the jungle and into the open. This dream was so real it terrified me, and it was as if they were trying to get me to stop and listen to them telling me something I wasn't yet aware of. But I wasn't prepared to stop and listen to them. These dinosaurs were making a crying sound as they ran after me. I seemed to be pushed out onto a wooden platform by them before I woke from the dream. And they were only about two feet tall, so they were babies.

Another night I dreamed of a lizard and he actually bit my ankle very hard, so hard that I jumped in my bed and quickly woke up. As I sat up, I grabbed my ankle and rubbed it. It had really bitten me, and I had been woken by its bite. Something was trying to awaken me to something greater than I knew. Was I actually slipping into other dimensions in these dreams? Because I was physically feeling the effects from the dreams. I still had the feeling of the bite from the lizard for a long time – or were some ancient memories being rekindled for me? Was my spirit trying to get in touch with me to remember my former lifetimes, or what I had to do in this world?

My days were long, but I was glad that Javier found himself an easy job and he was away from the house. Again, I was housebound; however, this time I didn't want to become too friendly with the neighbours. I had done that in Hastings Crossing and the old people enjoyed my visits. But it all got too much for me in the end. I needed some time to myself and away from the old.

Our new house was wonderful; I liked it very much. It was very modern and had a big yard, which I mowed and tended to. The yard was like the side of a mountain, and it wasn't easy to mow. I also washed the three cars, so I was still doing everyone else's work, but it filled in my days. That was one thing about me

– I wasn't lazy and I was rarely idle for too long. This new house kept me very busy. I decided to rearrange the existing rock garden, which was set around a man-made river with a pond. I set to work pulling it all apart and reassembling it. It was time-consuming but enjoyable, and I didn't know then I was grounding myself in the physical world, because my dreams were sending me off into higher dimensions on a spiritual level, and I wasn't aware of the necessity of grounding oneself during spiritual experiences; for that matter, I wasn't aware I was having spiritual experiences. Nonetheless, I liked being outdoors and with nature, and this work and nature gave me a sense of peace.

Chapter 18

Death And Poverty

In July 1990, two years after Uncle Mitch's death, we were summoned to Rosemont to see Aunty Connie because she hadn't been well. I will never forget the look on her face and her fears around her health. I wondered – did she feel death knocking on her door? Her grip on your hand was so tight. It was as if she was trying to not slide into some deep abyss. She grabbed each of us at intervals to see which one of us could save her from the darkness that awaited her, and she held each of our hands with such strength, like she knew she was going to die. She didn't want to let go. It was hard to watch her go through this. The hardest thing of all was how she'd physically let herself deteriorate. Her hair was long, grey and lifeless, and badly needed a cut and a colour. Her lovely white teeth were rotten, and she looked older than her years. She was only sixty-six.

A month after that day, we got news that Aunty Connie had died in hospital. Uncle Mitch was sixty-six and she was sixty-six. Both were sixty-six? There was another phenomenon: both were in their late sixties –

was there a curse put on this family, that no one would live to seventy?

Sure enough, there was another shock. Of course, Aunty Connie left all her fortune to an outsider, Oliver; the family house at the lake was gone forever from the family.

After the will was read out, there was speculation that Connie had been influenced by Oliver to leave him everything, her two houses and all her money. The family agreed that he was entitled to the house that they'd both been living in at Denton, but the family didn't agree that Oliver should get the family summer house at Sandy Lake. When Connie married Oliver, he was a beggar virtually off the street, and he'd gone to the Save the People Organisation for assistance and met my Aunty Connie. And over their marriage he'd never let her spend a penny of her money on herself. He couldn't deny her seeing the doctor, because she was a chronic diabetic. He had no option there; she had to have her insulin and other life-saving medicines. I felt he saw an opportunity in her for his own gain, and he knew she wasn't a well woman. Not only did she have diabetes, but she had a bad heart because she was born with a hole in her heart.

Connie had gone to the bottom of the barrel with Oliver, from an eloquent woman who had a spotless home to an old hag with a house that was very badly dirty, and we had to question why, because she had money. We suggested to Connie to get her hair cut and coloured and get her teeth fixed. There was no way we could get her to see, and she'd inform us that Oliver liked her that way.

After the will was read and everything was handed over to Oliver, he walked off with a very big fortune, because the properties in Rosemont had skyrocketed and the property at the lake on the waterfront had done likewise. Not too long after he'd squandered the whole lot of that fortune on women through reckless living. It seemed to be a fate in this family that a family member died early, and their money was given to outsiders, and then they lost the property and money.

My dad had told us it was said that Grandma squandered her fortune by giving away large amounts of property willed to her from Grandfather's estate that he'd built up over his lifetime before his death, and she had also given away lots of money to relatives. Grandma had also bailed my Uncle Mitch out of jail on occasions for fighting, and she'd finance his wild lifestyle. All these bad moves caused her to live a mega existence and a not-too-good lifestyle, even though she had a house to live in for free until she died, which had been willed to her by the Davies, the owners of the pit.

As my father told us this story I thought, *This is true.* But Grandma lived so poorly; she badly neglected herself. Her hair was long, straggly and grey. She too was a beautiful woman who ended up a lonely hag. She never looked after her health, and she wore black, poor-looking clothes that seemed long out of date. She too had rotten teeth in her mouth, and she wouldn't spend her money on helping herself. All she did was live in the past and in grief over the death of her husband and son, and used them as her excuse for her life.

Dad told us that there was a curse put on the Kinread family, especially the males, and that no male would live to see seventy. This curse had been in effect for the past two hundred years. At that time, I didn't understand such things about curses, nor could I see things like patterns in a family. I didn't have this knowledge. It would take many more years for me to understand our families' patterns and behaviours and in doing that, I myself would become part of the patterns and behaviours to fully understand them. Now there was only my dad left, and he vowed he'd never do the same thing that his family members had done so far; I couldn't imagine Mum allowing it anyway.

Around this time, I was really fed up with my mum, because she and Dad were fighting more often. Every time we went to visit them it was pitiful, and you could cut the tension in the house with a knife. All I could do was listen to her woes, because Javier and Dad would leave the room and go outside and sit on the back patio to talk so Dad could have a smoke, and that irritated Mum, because he wasn't supposed to smoke. Many times she would call me, and I'd have to run over to her, if I had the car, and comfort her, and listen to her woes. I couldn't tell her to get a life and stop complaining.

More news hit the family, and death struck again. This time in Spain: Javier's father died from cancer. No one knew he had cancer, and no one went over to his funeral, and furthermore, no one shed a tear for him. The only one to feel anything for him and his departure was Julian. Julian really did love his grandfather. At this time, Jerod experienced the death of a friend; his best mate, Reece, was killed while working for his father, doing a weekend job. Death seemed to be invading us.

Chapter 19

I Love The Theatre

There was an opportunity in December of 1990 to go and see a famous stage show. I wanted to see it really badly. I had gone to the theatre a few times with Javier. However, this show was outside of our hometown, in another state.

I spoke to my sister about the show and she wanted to go. So she arranged for her friend, Jillana, to go with her. I asked Javier if I could go and explained to him that I really wanted to go. He declined and I virtually begged him and convinced him to let me go, informing him I would be with my sister and her friend. So I was allowed to go, and my sister arranged the tickets, airfares and accommodation for the three of us. We were all excited.

Not long before we were to go, my sister told us that Jillana couldn't go and it would only be the two of us. That didn't worry me. However, Javier saw an opportunity – without my sister's friend going, he'd go. So he took her place and went with us. Nevertheless, I was very excited. This was my first interstate flight and it showed me I was a very adventurous person and proved to me this was my nature. I was supposed to travel. I had been telling Javier that when our boys left home and we were on our own, we should travel and live in different countries. That fishing village was still etched in my mind. I knew it was never his dream.

This flight increased my excitement to travel. We'd had a ride in a small four-seater plane on a holiday. However, this was a major flight. How was I going to like it?

The day came and we drove to Rosemont and parked at the airport. The place was abuzz. The travel atmosphere was getting into my body. On the plane, I loved it. I loved the take-off and the full experience and reminded Javier of travelling in later life.

We arrived at our destination and got a taxi to the hotel, where we had fun getting ready. We were running a bit late and we needed a taxi to the theatre. It was so exciting; we found a taxi and I said to the driver, 'To the theatre; don't spare the gas, and run the red lights.' I was so excited, so was my sister. We laughed a lot. Javier didn't, but he was there so he had to go with it.

My sister and I loved the show. We collected brochures and enjoyed the atmosphere. The next day, we spent the day walking around the markets and did the historical sites. A great day, and then home the next. I think Javier was a bit upset, because he sped home. I warned him a few times, 'You're speeding,' and he wouldn't listen to me. He should never have come with us; there was no indication of us doing anything other than seeing a show and walking the streets to enjoy the sights of the town. We weren't there for any other reason. He must have felt he'd wasted a weekend and his money.

He was booked for speeding and we went home. My sister got in her car and went and that was it. There were never any more interstate shows to go to.

Chapter 20

Work Opportunity

It was a whole year that I had stayed home, just filling in my days, doing nothing but housework and gardening. Jerod had also decided to do nursing as a career like Julian. He really wanted to go into economics; however, one of Julian's school friends, Barton, had advised him not to, so he decided to do nursing, which was good for us as well, because there were no fees until 1993, and he would have completed his course by then. So Jerod was off to university as well. Their lives were set.

In May of 1991, an opportunity presented itself in a pamphlet that was dropped off in our mailbox. It was a pamphlet on recruiting personal care workers. As I read it, I learned there was a free six-week course available to obtain a certificate in personal care. I was doing nothing at home, and the boys were hardly at home and didn't need me as much. I showed Javier the pamphlet and asked him if I could do the course. I was amazed when he agreed to it. I looked at him, surprised, and said, 'Thanks.'

Straight away, I enrolled in the course and did it. After the initial course was over, we were placed into various nursing homes or aged care facilities, called hostels, for work experience. Fortunately, I was sent to Mako Hostel at Linton. It was a brand-new facility; it had four units, with approximately ten bedrooms per unit. The facility was very plush, and it was carpeted throughout; each unit had a communal dining room and lounge room, and individual bedrooms and bathrooms combined for each resident. The units were sunny within, with sky roofs for natural light, and the place was beautifully landscaped with Australian plants. Each unit had an English name. I did my six-week work experience in Sunnyside Court, where I was trained by Carol, a lovely, jovial lady who was a touch sensitive. Carol was robust but agile on her feet and had a good heart towards the elderly; she was very good at training people. I thought she had a flair for teaching.

I fitted in so well and I loved the place and the old people. They were so grateful for the smallest of things, and they seemed to love me. The manager, Mr Gordon, offered me a job there after my six weeks' work experience. I went home to tell Javier the good news about scoring a job at this hostel.

On arriving home, my excitement was great, and I had to contain it and not be too over enthusiastic. I rushed into the house and before he could think, I said, 'Javier, I have the opportunity to work at that facility I've been doing work experience at.'

Without a breath, I said, 'We can save the money I make, and when the boys are off our hands, which won't be long because they're getting older, we can travel. Remember how I used to tell you, "When the boys leave us, let's go and live in different countries for a couple of months"?'

He was stunned and speechless, because I'd got in quickly before he could think about what I'd said. My enthusiasm was high, even though I tried to keep it down, and in my mind, I knew this idea was too good for him to pass up. As luck had it, he bought it, and he agreed to me working there. However, he had a few questions that had to be answered. I acknowledged each question with thought and discretion.

'What's the place like?' he asked.

Being careful with my words in order to not lose this opportunity, I said, 'Well, there are only women there because there are only cooks and personal carers, and personal carers are people who wash and clean the old people.'

'Oh,' he quipped, as I continued on, 'And there's lady cleaners as well. But my job will be cooking in the afternoons.'

I watched his face and waited. Again, I reminded him of the benefits in the long run of me having this job, and stated, 'We can travel, and my job is only for three days a week, for four hours each day.' I smiled, waiting in anticipation.

Javier put his head down and hesitated. He could see I was so excited, and we could do with the extra money, even before we decided to travel. Then he agreed. I hugged him in my excitement, and he asked, 'How will you get to work? You've got no car.'

'Don't worry, I will learn the bus times, and I'll go by bus.' I had thought all this out well in advance, and there was nothing I was leaving out. Somehow, I had to have this job, and I got it. I took the job, and so I started my work there as an afternoon shift cook with some personal caring.

On 7th June, 1991, I began working at Mako Hostel. Years later I found out that 'mako' was the name for a type of shark and the shark is about authority. Mako was an institution for the old. There I would face lots of people in authority, and who liked to wield authority. Sharks teach us to respect these people, and to understand the roles they play in authority. I had a problem with authority and hated it.

Nonetheless, I loved the job, and it felt great going to work every day. I didn't want to miss a day, ever. There, my heart was opening up, and for the first time, I found that love dwelled inside of me. I had so much love to give to these old people. Feelings of overwhelming love gripped me – the same loving feelings I had for my children when they were little. These feelings I felt for my children, my nephews and niece, or for the animals we had as pets. This hidden love inside of me was resurfacing, and it made me very affectionate. The same affection I had towards my sons, I could now give to the old.

The dementia wing was being built when I started my six-week work experience there. I noticed some of the men building it. They were different to the men I knew in appearance and seemed more bohemian and unsettled type of people. This dementia section was soon up and running and called Rose House. I used to go to work early in the afternoon, around 1pm, but the job started at 3:30pm, so I did voluntary work there. I worked with the people I once feared as a child. I'd feared these people right up into my early adulthood.

Suddenly, there was no fear of these people. It was as if I was seeing things from a wider perspective. They were mentally challenged due to dementia. I loved them and could tolerate their endless repetitive questioning. I had to get used to their ways and their mindsets; that was the challenge for me as a carer. With time I was good at caring for the ones with dementia. All over the facility I had a wonderful rapport with the aged, on all levels. The supervisor, Ruby, encouraged me to think about working in the field of Activities, and doing hands-on stimulation work with these people. I loved that work, and I'd go into the dementia section as often as I could to learn how to work with these people and help out.

As a cook, I was so happy, and like a whirlwind, literally, whirling around the tables serving the residents in my unit in Primrose Cottage. I remember one of our residents, Maggie, who suffered from early-onset dementia, kept saying to her husband Lance, 'There's a wind coming in and out of here. Where is it coming from?' Lance looked at me and I'd smile back at him as I heard her words. He'd lovingly look at Maggie; place his hand on her back and say, 'It's only Chris rushing past you.' I was so happy with my job; I'd practically dance around the tables.

This job brought out so much happiness, a happiness I never felt existed in me, and in that feeling, I was always laughing and smiling at work. Those were my best days. But that elation upset some people at work and caused me a lot of trouble with work colleagues, because no one could understand why I was so radiant. I too didn't know exactly why I was so joyous. Effie was the most horrified at my behaviour;

she worked in the main office, thank goodness, and she only got to see me now and then. Try as she may, she couldn't understand my enthusiasm for life, and I felt I irritated her. It wasn't intentional happiness to irritate others. Effie wasn't nasty about it; she just couldn't understand me, or why I acted the way I did. To be truthful, I couldn't understand my joy and the overwhelming feelings of love emanating through me. I was ecstatically happy, and I could show great elation to the residents on all levels: the infirm and crippled, those with dementia, the mentally challenged, those diseased with all kinds of skin conditions and other internal diseases. I wasn't afraid of those covered in sores and skin lesions. There were no barriers to my love towards these people. But as a child, thinking such people were unclean, I would have run away from them in fear or walked across streets to avoid them, so they wouldn't touch me and pass something on to me. Back then, I feared their germs so much. In this job, germs didn't enter my mind while I was caring for them. All these changes came into my life once I moved to Dawson Hill, and I started having those memorable dreams.

As a child, if I saw a drunk person, a physically handicapped person, or a mentally challenged person, I'd be afraid of them. But it was a fear out of my own ignorance of such people. At Mako, I faced those fears. I learned that many of the aged lose their personal hygiene for many reasons. I must have been with them to break my fears and ignorance. We have to face our fears and our ignorance to solve them, and many of us are not aware of this, or aware of what dwells within us.

Little did I know then, I was on the threshold of facing all my own shadows that had been deeply buried in my subconscious mind. Unbeknown to me, in the future there would be one man who would have the key to unlock that chess box of mystery, and I would end up being placed in a seven-and-a-half-year hell with him, whereby I'd be in a constant battle with him to tell me the truth. But it wasn't his truth I wanted. It was all the keys he had within him to unlock me. It was my own truth I would be seeking.

At this facility, I met many different kinds of people from all walks of life. The facility had a diversity of aged people. The staff were diverse as well.

The past re-entered my life. I was still working in Primrose Cottage. Next door was the unit Corner House; directly to the side of Primrose Cottage, I saw this lady cleaning the floor. Moving further into that unit and towards her, I said, 'Hi, I know you – you're Camilla,' as I smiled at her.

She stopped washing the floor and looked up at me. 'Chris, my God, it's you.'

I said, 'Yes, fancy meeting you here after all these years. At last we've caught up again.'

'When was it I last saw you?' she asked.

'I met you at your wedding to Pepe and we last saw each other at my Jerod's christening in 1974,' I informed her.

She acknowledged it. 'Yes, I know now. And what happened to you? Are you still with Javier?' she asked, smiling as she leaned on her mop. As I answered her and looked at her, I realised she hadn't changed a bit. She still seemed so tall, with a big bone structure. She had no fat on her, and her large teeth filled her mouth. Her brown eyes shone like stars and they made her look so pretty. She was so excited and had a hundred and one questions for me.

I answered her by saying, 'I'm still with Javier. And you, are you still with Pepe?'

Sadly, she looked down, twirled the mop in the bucket of water, and stated, 'Yes, but I'm not happy with Pepe. We're having problems. I've been thinking of separating from him,' she admitted, and all her glow had left her face.

'Oh! I'm so sorry to hear that, Camilla,' I expressed with my own feelings of regret. Because I too was in the same boat with Javier.

As if she'd caught my sadness for her, she explained, 'No, it's been coming for a while, Pepe knows it's inevitable.'

Although I was in the same predicament and frame of mind, I didn't tell her about my marriage issues, or how I felt the same way about my marriage. I was like that: no one knew anything about my marriage. Everyone thought Javier and I were happily married. I had to bide my time to open up, because I had too many trust issues with women. Camilla started that day as a cleaner, but she wouldn't be a cleaner for too long there.

In my unit, Primrose Cottage, I had a lovely couple, Vera and Evan, as residents. I liked them so much, even though they were very set in their ways. I'd noticed that with the aged: it had to be their way or no way, and they didn't like change. I realised this very quickly. Nonetheless, being a very diplomatic person, I allowed them their choices. If I could suggest another alternative,

I did so, in the politest of ways. My grandma had done well in teaching me to be polite. Too well, as a matter of fact, and much to my own detriment.

Vera wasn't well herself, but she'd dedicated her last years to her husband Evan. She'd been his carer since he'd had a stroke years ago. Unfortunately, she had to move to this care facility and leave their home, because caring for him was too much for her. She was a very dutiful wife to him. Nonetheless, his deterioration worsened due to Parkinson's disease, as well as being a stroke victim. My role was to take the burden off of them or from the spouse, in their case as a couple. However, my role, and the roles of all the personal carers who attended to them, was very difficult for Vera to accept, and to give up her caring role to him was too much for her to bear. We all understood her and tried to alleviate her distress in that regard. We reassured her that we weren't taking over her role; we were helping her. Many of the elderly as couples felt guilty if they couldn't continue playing out their roles to the end. I was very close to this couple. As I was to many of the other residents in my house. I guess I was more tolerant of Vera and she was of me, too.

I was off work in the morning and my shift started in the afternoon. At home, I walked over our little bridge that crossed the man-made river in my garden to go to the clothesline. I stopped suddenly and heard the words, 'Chris, will you promise to take care of Evan for me?' Those words really stopped me in my tracks. I stood there for a moment and wondered what that was all about. I knew whose voice it was: Vera's. I recognised it and her energy. I responded, 'Yes, I will take care of him.' Then her energy left me. I was alone on the bridge and there was no one else around. That afternoon when I went to work, I was told Vera had passed over that day, around 12 noon. That was the time I had a visit from her. I never doubted the other side, and I did care for Evan until he had to leave us and go into a nursing home.

When that day came, it was so sad. I will never forget his face as he cried, and I watched the tears flow down his face. With us he felt safe and secure. There was nothing I could do to stop it; he had to go to a nursing home. There, the care was better for him, but the environment would not be so personal. Evan was never the same person after Vera's death. He never smiled and I often found him with tears streaming down his cheeks. All I could do was sit with him and smile, a smile that somehow understood him in his loneliness. All these people I had encountered left some wonderful memories with me.

A new resident came to the hostel. Her name was Ting. On meeting her I wondered what she was doing here, because she was so happy and full of life. I thought, This is not the place for her. Sometimes before my afternoon shift, I would visit some of the clients outside of the dementia unit. As I visited Ting, we became closer, and she informed me that her eyesight had caused her to come and live here. She felt insecure on her own, because the love of her life had died. She kept a picture of him on her bedside table, but it was a picture of a very young man in a trench coat. He seemed like an agent out of a *Bond* movie, and just as handsome.

As we got closer, I found out that Ting loved any form of beauty. She really liked my company and was so pleased to know me, and told me I was like a breath of fresh air that passed through her life and everyone else's here at Mako. She continually told me I was so beautiful, but I couldn't see it. She stared at me when I entered, as if some goddess had just walked into her room, and she'd say, 'I bet you were so beautiful when you were a young girl. You should have gone into modelling.' Then she'd turn away from me, as if she was disappointed that I didn't do that. I'd told her that was one of my dreams, but I never fulfilled it. All I could do was smile at her and shrug my shoulders. 'You've truly missed your calling,' she'd impart on me, looking at me with her loving eyes and serious face.

Her words made me sad, because I did miss out on so many opportunities due to not having guidance from my parents or self-knowledge on how to do things. I realised I'd married too young and didn't give myself a chance to experience life and find myself and my talents. It was too late to pine over the past, so I kept smiling. I would never put any of my sadness on others, especially these old people, because from the stories they'd told me, they had already endured enough of their own personal sadness and grief.

Ting wasn't the only one who imparted words of my beauty onto me. It came from Javier as well, and many others in years to come. But I just couldn't see my own beauty when I looked in the mirror. Little did I know, looking in the mirror wasn't the place to see it. I didn't realise my beauty was an invisible beauty.

Even though we fought and Javier knew I detested him, he still constantly told me how beautiful I was. So did my Uncle Mitch. Every time Uncle Mitch saw me, he'd say, 'Chris was the one who got the family beauty. God bugger me, she is so beautiful.' I'd giggle and just look at him and think, *Where is this beauty?*

Chapter 21

My Father's Mother And Dementia

Grandma Kinread died in 1975. She'd had dementia; I never knew what that was back then, and now I was working with people with dementia. I thought about all those years my mum and dad lived with her. They'd given up their lives for her. She'd told them she'd only live another two years in 1951, and she died in 1975. Grandma had interfered in my parents' lives and caused them many problems. I often wondered if she ever realised what she did to them. I know I felt trapped by their unspoken feelings – and here I was trapped in a marriage with a man I don't love. Why was I repeating a similar life to my parents? They were induced to stay with my grandma, and Dad didn't want to give up a good thing, like free rent. He'd virtually forced Mum to look after Grandma when she'd become bedridden. Mum accepted what Dad wanted her to do. It was done under protests, growls and complaining, mainly to me, but she did it for him so he could keep Grandma at the big old farmhouse. Was I going to end up in a similar situation, stuck with a man for security?

Dad never took any responsibility for the care of his mother – that was all handed over to my mum. I don't think Dad realised the task he'd set upon Mum. Mum, too, was playing the martyr, which never paid off in the end. I learned that the one who did the most was the one who got kicked around like a dog, never thanked, appreciated or valued for their worth.

I remembered going to the nursing home to visit my grandma. On one of my visits I was told she'd lost her faculties and was lost in her childhood. I had no idea what the nursing staff or Mum was talking about. Grandma Kinread was always talking about her sister, who'd gone to Canada to live. But I was told she was talking about her in the now, and that she was going down the street looking for her dog.

Now I understood what was happening to my grandma, and that she was experiencing dementia. On my visits to her, I could hardly recognise my grandma, especially just before her death; I had to read the overhead name card to see if it was her.

The day of her funeral, in the church, I had a strange feeling. This feeling had happened to me before during a funeral service. I laughed inwardly; it's like it's a joke, that we all get so caught up over death. I thought to myself, *My grandma isn't in that box, not at all. Why is everyone so sad for her? She's gone elsewhere – I don't know where, but it's beyond here.* Besides losing Grandma, her death turned out to be a great family get-together. That's one good thing about a funeral or a wedding: it brings families together.

Grandma was old, and she had put herself into her bed many years ago. She'd given up on life, and she

119

lived a sad life, mourning the deaths of her husband and son. I'm sure she was waiting out her time to die. I truly believe that there is a time when we are called back home. To me, home isn't here, it's somewhere else; I don't know where, but it's definitely not here.

All my cousins and I had unconsciously dressed in brown, and our beloved Aunty Connie was there, even though she was frail herself and not well with her diabetes. We were so glad to see her; she'd changed so much, from a beautiful woman to a dishevelled old hag of a woman. Nonetheless, we all still loved her.

In Mum and Dad's house where we held the wake, she asked us, as we all gathered around her like we did as children, 'Do you girls realise you all wore Grandma's favourite colour today?'

We all smiled, and Gerry said, 'How, Aunty?'

'Well, you're all wearing the colour brown,' she informed us. We looked at each other; sure enough, we were all in brown clothes. We giggled. Somehow, we knew that Grandma would be pleased with us.

Out of my cousins, Hope was like me; she knew things beyond this world, but she feared such things, too. But all would open up for her in later life. She tried to suppress it, but you can't – eventually you have to face it.

I was in this facility caring for the elderly. Was I there to understand my grandma and her grieving life? Do grief, shame, guilt and unresolved issues in our lives result in the deterioration of our minds?

Chapter 22

Julian Marries Gerry

Living in Dawson Hill, Julian was wanting to go out with his new male friends, Mitchell and Art, who he was going to university with. This was only natural. Julian was in his third year of nursing; I could see he was changing, and I could see he was feeling different towards Gerry. It was obvious he wanted to cool things off. Julian was trying to distance himself from her. Gerry felt it too.

I'd gone upstairs to the bathroom and caught him and Gerry at his bedroom door. They must have been in quite a heated conversation. I stopped, not meaning to barge in. I looked at them both; they looked back at me with troubled, almost worried looks. I smiled and continued on into the bathroom, not wanting to interfere.

When Javier came home that evening, Julian approached us. We were both sitting in the family room on the settee, watching TV. Julian said, 'Mum and Dad, Gerry and I have something to tell you.'

I smiled and asked, 'What is it?', as I looked at them. They glanced at Javier; he wasn't as happy.

Julian and Gerry sat on the other settee to our right. Nervously, Julian said, 'Mum and Dad, Gerry and I are going to have a baby.'

In my excitement, forgetting myself and the circumstances around them having a baby, I said, 'Oh, Julian and Gerry, congratulations, a baby.' I was genuinely happy for them. Julian wasn't happy. He was looking very apprehensive, but Gerry was as happy as I was. However, diverting my eyes to Javier, I saw he wasn't so happy either. The look on his face wasn't a look of joy for our first grandchild.

I asked, 'When will the baby be born?'

Gerry answered me, smiling, her eyes beaming with joy as she looked at Julian for reassurance: 'February.'

'Oh, lovely, our first grandchild.'

Then Julian calmed. He dropped his fears, placed his arm around Gerry, looked at her and said, 'Yes, and it will be alright, won't it, possum?' – something he affectionately called her. We were all more settled about it. The next thing to do was to arrange a marriage.

After the initial surprise and joy for me, I did wonder, though, because Gerry was on the Pill; she didn't want to have any children for a while, then strangely, she was pregnant. I wondered: did she get herself pregnant because she felt Julian was changing towards her? She had to have made a snap decision and gone off the Pill, I reasoned. Later on, I found out that she did go off the Pill – she'd told Julian she was developing a rash and couldn't stay on it. But I knew that was not true. She'd fallen pregnant to keep Julian.

Other truths came out as Julian confided in us when Gerry wasn't around. He told us that Gerry's mother said if Julian didn't marry her, Gerry would be registering their child under her maiden name of Farrow. This was really bad news, and it was very deceitful of her family to say such a cruel and threatening thing to such a lovely and too-kind-hearted boy. They knew Julian was a softie, and Gerry knew how to hurt him or manipulate him to her benefit. It made me wonder: what was Gerry's motive? Because later on, there would be a cooling-off on her part towards Julian, and he would suffer by her and by her mother Gertrude.

Jerod wasn't too happy about his brother having to get married so young, but there was nothing that could be done about it. Jerod's girlfriend, Chantal, who was also training to be a nurse at the university Jerod attended, was concerned for Julian as well, and her facial expression showed me that she'd never do that to Jerod – become pregnant before marrying. I liked Chantal so much, and she and I got on so well. She was more affectionate than Gerry towards me. Gerry was a very wiry girl, country-bred. She was the type of girl who rode the farm horses and enjoyed a real farm life; having been involved with the animals, she wasn't very feminine in her dress sense. Her long blonde hair fell around a strong, square jawline. She seemed to lack common sense, but she was highly intelligent. It was nothing for her to score in the nineties in major examinations. Both her parents were teachers and both she and her brother, Hudson, were well-tutored. Chantal was a softer personality, and a little chubby and cuddly with it. She oozed affection. She also had long blonde hair with a fringe that set off her pretty, small, round face, and her soft brown eyes made her look almost angelic. Julian had asked Jerod to be his best man; Jerod accepted. Mitchell and Art were his groomsmen.

The day came for Julian and Gerry to get married. They were married at 4pm in a park in Dawson Hill. Gerry didn't want a religious church wedding; she organised to have a female celebrant marry them. Gerry and her family and friends came all the way from Spencer Shire to Dawson Hill; we didn't have as far to go, just a ten-minute drive into town. The 31st of August, the day they chose to get married, was a perfect, sunny day. It was very strange, because they married on the day Julian was supposed to be born. The following day was his twenty-first birthday – the 1st of September, 1991.

It was a wonderful wedding, and the park was in its full splendour with beautifully manicured lawns and seasonal flowers that added colour to the magnificence of the day. It was good even though I'd forgotten the boys' flowers for their lapels, much to Gertrude's horror, but they were just flowers. The loveliest part of the wedding was having all the family together. For some reason, I beamed. I didn't care what Javier thought; I just mixed with everyone and chatted away to men, women, boys and girls, and laughed. I had a ball that day. I was truly in my own power and felt very strong within myself. Furthermore, it was mostly only family, so Javier wasn't too threatened by the crowd. He was always comfortable around the family. Unfortunately – and not going against Gerry – I felt someone in our family was marrying the wrong person, and another was being trapped into an early marriage by a pregnancy.

The next day, we had another big party at our house to celebrate Julian's twenty-first birthday. Julian wanted to do that. He delayed his own honeymoon to be with us and his friends on his twenty-first birthday. It turned out to be a great day. I loved seeing my boys together with their friends; they were so happy and mucked around and tormented each other, playing tricks on one another. That would gradually stop, because Julian was now married.

The following day, he and Gerry went off on their honeymoon. When Julian returned from his honeymoon, he came home and took his gear from the house. It really hit me: I'd lost him forever, and he wasn't coming back to live with us. He was my first son to leave the nest, and I felt so much sadness in losing him. However, I felt their marriage was not secure.

That same month I turned forty, on the twenty-fifth of September. In Australia, a fortieth was usually a big celebration, but not for me. I had friends from work, but I wasn't allowed to have my friends in my life or bring them into our family circle, because Javier couldn't handle me having friends. I felt like I had no friends, but I did: I had lots of friends, and some lovely ones. My guests were Julian and Gerry, her parents, my parents, and Jerod and Chantal. It was a lovely night in a very nice restaurant, but it wasn't the party I'd wanted.

What I'd missed out on not having a party, I received at work, because Camilla and other friends gave me lots of wonderful presents. I knew then that I was well-liked by people. My most precious gift, though, was from Emere. Emere was the supervisor in the dementia unit. She'd given me a small daily diary and a card with the words, 'Dear Christ, I hope you can use this gift, and I wish you all the best, lots of love from Emere.' Emere had opened up a remembrance of my youth when I used to write in my diaries. Her gift made me realise it was time to do this again. Deep within me, I knew I should write and keep a daily journal. She called me Chris when she spoke to me, but when she wrote my name on her card, she'd put 'Christ'. I don't know why.

My home life had to be separated from work. But there was a new lady at work, whom I was getting on well with: Kay, who was working in Corner House unit next to my unit, Primrose Cottage. She'd asked me to call her at home at night-time to chat. Because she was divorced, she had no man to answer to. It was different for her, but my other friends like Peggy and Camilla were married, and they didn't need to talk to me after work hours. I decided to call Kay one night after dinner. As I went to the phone to make the call, Javier asked, 'Who are you calling?'

'Kay, a new lady from work. She asked me to give her a ring,' I explained.

He stopped and said nastily, 'Don't call her. People don't want to be bothered with you.'

I looked at him disbelievingly and said, 'That's not true. She asked me to call her.'

'Well, don't call her. She doesn't want to be your friend,' he informed me.

I got so upset by his remarks and called her. I defied him, but it was hard because he sat near me and listened to our conversation. Afterwards, he snarled at me and walked off. It was getting more difficult being in that house with him. Javier was so fearful of me being friendly with other people and neglecting him – or maybe he was afraid I might wise up to him through others.

Around this time, I decided to buy myself a special gift. It was a beautiful porcelain unicorn, a very expensive piece sculpted by a young lady from the North Coast. On seeing it in the shop, I instantly loved it and had to have it. I lay-byed it for myself and paid it off slowly. That unicorn figurine sat on my floor, and every time I felt sad, I would go to it and sit with it and stare into its almost-alive eyes. Its beauty and design were exquisite; I felt an inner peace looking into its face, and it did hold a magic within it.

Javier decided he wanted to go to where I worked to check it out for himself. He did this a couple of times to reassure himself that I wasn't being misled by anyone there, and to see for himself the people I worked with. He hated how I was so friendly to the elderly and the staff. He said, 'People here are not truthful, and they are just pretending to like each other.' I looked at him, shook my head and thought, *You can't see anything nice in this world.*

I calmly said, 'Javier, that's not true, and they are lovely people. How can you think that?' He had no concept of what it was like being with the elderly; they seemed to bring out an enormous amount of love within the group, and it wasn't just me who loved them. It was all the staff, and fifty staff members can't all be wrong. To me, all the staff members were genuinely happy there, and happy with their work with the elderly. Many times, Javier tried to stop me from working, but I refused to stop. He wasn't going to tell me what to do anymore. He'd controlled my life long enough. I'd taken it to keep the peace, but now that Julian was married and Jerod was becoming more independent, I didn't need to obey him. I wasn't going to sit at home and die internally while I waited for him to return home from work. And what for? There was nothing between us, our marriage was dead; so we continued to fight, due to his fears.

I still didn't have a car, and I was catching the bus to work; however, one of the new ladies, Glenda, found out I just lived down the road from her, so she offered to take me home after our shift. I could have gotten a lift with her into work, but I wanted to do my voluntary work in the dementia unit and visit other clients in the hostel before my afternoon shift started. Nonetheless, I was so grateful to get a lift home; it saved me waiting for a bus in the evening.

So after our shift she drove me home – however, Glenda was a motor mouth and a compulsive chatterer. It was as if she couldn't help herself; there was no coming up for air at times. Her conversations were based around her family. By the time we got to my house, she was still wound up after a twenty-minute drive, still going a hundred and one miles an hour chatting. At my house, she pulled up in her car and actually turned off the motor and still kept speaking to me. I could not get away from her, and being the polite adult I was, I stayed and listened to her, knowing full well there would be hell when I got into the house. I couldn't tell her about my marital problems, and if I did, she would have told me to tell him to get a life.

When I eventually got away from her and went into the house, it was on. Javier accused me of everything, of being out the front of the house with this woman, like boyfriend and girlfriend. That really threw me, and I wondered how he could say that about two women, for goodness' sake. This hurt me, him saying such things. I explained, 'Javier, she's a married woman and has children. We were just talking about her children, and I can't be rude and say I have to go.'

But he was not happy with that answer, and said, 'The neighbours probably think you've got a boyfriend.' It was too much for me to take. Sometimes I'd just sink into myself and go off and do something in the house to avoid him, but he'd keep bringing it up, and I would calmly say to him, 'I will try and get away from her and come straight in to the house.' I acted calmly with him because I didn't want to lose my job, and I'd say anything to keep the peace and that job, because it was far better than wasting my life in that house.

Unfortunately, Javier was very good at demoralising me, and I lacked confidence in those days; he had me so downtrodden. I wondered if people did like me, so I actually asked some people at work if I was bothering them, and they laughed and asked me why I'd asked such a silly question. I couldn't tell them why, of course. I wasn't a bother, and I was very well-liked by all. But I hadn't had friends since my school days, and I didn't know how to act with friends, or be a friend. Not long after this, Javier bought himself an old car and I got to use our newer car. So now I was able to drive myself to work and come home by myself, and there were no worries for Javier.

Javier's family had stopped coming to visit us ages ago, after their father went to Spain to live, and we too had seemed to move away from them. With no one visiting us, I realised how alone and isolated I was. The only people who came to our home were Len, Javier's friend, and his new wife Vera. They'd visit us at our house or we'd occasionally go out with them. But I never regarded them as my friends, only as Javier's friends. They were really the only ones who stayed with us, and for some reason, unbeknown to me, his other friends came and left us, with no explanation. It was a sad time in the home, and sometimes I felt like the world had left me. I was starting to get stifled and smothered, and my freedom seemed to be a non-event. I had no one at all in my family or his family to talk to. I was been isolated from the new people I was meeting at work and felt like I was going through some depression. However, I always managed to shake it off. By accepting where I was at, I had the ability to cope. This was my gift: coping under whatever strain life offered me. I'd face it and deal with it. But Javier's behaviour was making me want to separate from him.

There was greater pressure now Julian was gone. I really missed him. I was happy for him, but sad also that I didn't get to see him every day; but deep down I think I was just sad for myself. Jerod was at Chantal's house more often, so there was only Javier and me most days. I think Jerod was sick of the arguments and games that went on in the house, and those were pretty awful at times. Many times, Javier accused me of letting the house go and told me the house was a pigsty. Because I was working, sometimes things slipped by for a couple of days, so he had me convinced in my naivety that the house was a pigsty. I believed him. I had to ask others if this was true.

I asked Chantal, 'Do you think the house is like a pigsty?'

She diverted her eyes to Javier, knowing not to let him hear her, and said quietly, 'No, Chris, it's beautiful, why do you ask?' She knew why, because she stared straight at him.

I said, 'Javier thinks it is, now I am working.'

She sweetly smiled and cuddled into me and said, 'No, Chris.' She was so reassuring, such a lovely girl, and we were very close. She was like a daughter to me, and often we'd sit on the lounge and talk for ages. I'd cuddle her, or she'd lie on my lap and I'd stroke her lovely long blonde hair. We had a lovely bond.

Chapter 23

The Christmas Party

My friendship was growing with Camilla, Kay and Peggy. We all got on so well and between the four of us we had lots of fun, which included our clients – our good times made the clients happy, too. It was early December and the staff Christmas party was being held at Mario's Restaurant in Petersham. I wore my favourite black dress, with a green-and-pink chiffon top in an off-the-shoulder design. I loved this dress and told Javier it was the dress I wanted to be buried in when I died. In those days, I often talked about my death and how I wanted my body to be disposed of. I didn't want to be buried in the ground; I told Javier I wanted to be buried out at sea in a glass coffin so I could look out and see the sea and the sea life around me, which made him and the boys laugh. But death never seemed to worry me. To me it was a natural occurrence in the process of life.

This dress was stunning, and there was a story behind it. I'd bought it and never showed it to Gema, and when I went down to the in-laws' house, Gema greeted me, all excited. As I entered the house, she grabbed my arm and pulled me off to her bedroom, saying, 'Come, Chris, see what I've bought.'

'What is it?' I asked, as she giggled, and I followed her.

'It's a dress.'

'Oh, nice.' I knew she loved nice clothes, especially now she was older.

We entered her bedroom and she said, 'Sit, Chris. This is the most stunning dress I have ever bought.' She was bubbling with excitement as she opened her wardrobe. We were both laughing, and then she pulled out an identical dress to mine, though hers was white.

'Gema, that's amazing. When did you buy that dress?' I asked, shocked, touching the dress with my eyes bulging. I couldn't believe it.

'Two days ago,' she said, wondering why I wasn't as excited as she was.

'Gema, two days ago, I bought the same dress, but in black,' I said as I stared at her, nodding my head in disbelief that we both picked the same dress, in different towns. She was surprised, too. I said, 'Are we that connected?'

She smiled and said, 'Yes, we are.'

Gema too would connect spiritually in her later life, but not in a good way. Her connection would frighten her, leaving her bewildered and afraid of her opening.

Those dresses had a history. I remembered when we first wore them together to a Spanish ball that all Javier's family attended. Javier and I were invited by his parents to go to this ball, and so we drove down to his parents' house and left our car at their place, going in my father-in-law's car. On the way to the ball, Javier looked at me and said, 'Tonight you don't leave my side. You sit with me all night.' I looked at him and my eyes asked him, Why? He looked away and never answered my questioning eyes. To divert from me, he started to talk to his father. By saying that, he deflated me instantly. I felt so down, whereas I had felt so pretty before, and he'd told me at home that I looked beautiful. So did Julian and Jerod.

At the venue, I guess he was worried that I would go from his side and talk to his family. So there I was, beautiful and trapped. That night, of course, his brothers and sisters were over at another table, and they kept beckoning me to go over. I had to shake my head to say no, and I directed my eyes at him to explain why I couldn't move from his side. Later, Gema asked me why I didn't go over to their table. I told her that Javier wanted me to stay with him, and she said, 'Ah! That bastard, I thought so.' She knew why.

Sometimes Gema got pissed off with her family. I think if she could have, she would have told them off many times in regard to me. She was more like my big sister than my little sister-in-law and she was feisty. But she too knew her limits in that household. She made me laugh by calling her own family 'fucking wogs', with 'dago mentality'.

'Gema, that's not nice,' I said.

'You don't know them, Chris,' she said. Seriously, she was right; I didn't know them or understand their mentality. I didn't know what Javier was worried about, because I was with his family, and what could I do with them? They were his brothers and sisters.

Nonetheless, out of the past and back in the moment.

The Christmas party was wonderful fun. Kay couldn't come because she couldn't get anyone to mind her children. So I hung around with Camilla and Peggy. Well, we laughed, cuddled and joked, and I felt like a free woman. I'd left Javier to talk to Camilla's husband, Pepe, so we women could have fun. We had the best time ever. Camilla, Peggy and I entertained ourselves. I didn't think of Javier for a moment. Occasionally, I glanced over his way; he was busy talking. The night was great, then Javier started to complain to me that he was sick, and he wanted to go home. This wasn't the first time he'd done this to me. He'd started to do this often when we went out.

I looked at him and asked, 'Are you really sick?'

'Yes, I am,' he stated, with a painful, snarling face.

I sighed and knew if I didn't go, he'd be upset. So I said, 'Okay, I'll tell everyone I am leaving.'

He snapped, 'You don't have to do that.'

I stood my ground and said, 'But I do, it's polite to.' I quickly ran around and told everyone I had to go.

'Why, Chris?' Camilla asked.

'Javier is sick,' I announced.

'Well, tell him to go home and you'll come later,' she told me casually.

I placed my hand to my heart and said, 'No, I couldn't do that, he'd kill me.'

She looked at him and said, 'I understand. Bloody wogs.' I laughed, because she was one. But to her, when they put shit out on others, they were 'wogs'.

So Javier and I left. I felt really elated and happy, because I'd had one of the best times ever. We went to our car and I was bubbling with happiness. I decided

135

to drive us home. All seemed okay with Javier, until we got close to Pembletown Shopping Centre, and there he turned on me. He was like a mad man. He accused me of being a slut. 'You slut, you slut,' he suddenly proclaimed to me.

I looked at him and at the road, and said, 'Javier, what are you saying? I did nothing; I just talked to the women there.' His eyes were mad, like he had a demon in him. Then he grabbed me as I drove the car. I screamed out, 'Javier, what are you doing?'

He stated, 'You think you're something special – well, you're not. You're a slut.'

By now I was frightened. I tried to pacify him, saying, 'I don't know what I've done wrong. I was only having fun with the ladies and that's all.' With that, he grabbed my favourite dress and ripped it off my back and tore it to shreds as I drove. I drove the rest of the way home naked from the waist up holding the strands up over my breasts to cover them. I cried and felt fearful of him, and worried that he might hit me next time. He grabbed my throat and shook me as I drove. I was speechless by then and just drove.

We reached the house, he opened the garage door, and I parked the car in the garage. Then I got out of the car and ran out of the garage to our back steps and into the house. I left him and ran, scared for my life. I didn't know what to do or where to go. I turned in circles in the lounge room. I wanted to hide, but where? Where could I hide? The garage door shut; he was coming. I heard his footsteps coming up the back steps and I was terrified, so much so that I whimpered. I went and stood behind the lounge room door. I waited and wondered, would he hit me? He was in a rage. I hadn't seen his face like this for a while, not since Len and Celia came to our house in Hastings Crossing and he and Len went to the pub to talk. Later, Len returned and took Celia and their children. We never saw them ever again. Something had clicked in Javier's brain. He wasn't a safe man to be around. I moved from behind the door and waited. I froze as he entered the lounge room. I wanted to faint. He must have seen the panic in my eyes, and he came closer.

'Javier, I didn't do anything wrong. I have never done anything to hurt you,' I whispered softly, with meaning and truth in my words. Somehow, with me expressing those words, he backed off. We went to our bedroom, and there I put on some clothes and he changed out of his good clothes. But I didn't feel safe. He had to go to the toilet, and he took his time there. I wondered: *Should I stay, or should I go?* In a split second I was off. I ran out of the house and made my escape. I opened the garage door as quietly as possible, got into the car and, with shaking hands, put the key in the ignition and turned it on. The motor roared and I drove like a maniac out of the garage – but where could I go? I drove around Dawson Hill. I had to go somewhere. So I went to his mother's house. I had never done this before, and never told anyone in my family what Javier was really like. They all believed our marriage was perfect and we had no problems. But that night, another side to our marriage was revealed.

On reaching my mother-in-law's house, I drove into their driveway and sat and pondered. I cried, which moved into sobs. It puzzled me to think how Javier couldn't believe that I had never done anything to hurt him. I'd never betrayed him in any way. I'd only been a good wife and mother and done my best. It was a hot night, but my body was cold with fear and sadness. I rubbed my shoulders, and then slowly emerged from the car. I closed the door quietly and walked up to their front door. I felt dazed and wondered, Is this a bad nightmare? But no – I was shivering; it was real.

The family was still up. I walked in. Javier's youngest brother and the baby of the family, Josico, approached me. 'Chris, what's up?' he asked. I couldn't speak, I was in shock. He said, 'Sit, Chris, and tell me, is Javier alright?'

I nodded, and his mother asked him something in Spanish. He told her off. I said, 'Javier and I were out. I didn't do anything wrong and he went off. I don't know why.'

I looked to Josico for answers. He turned to his mother and said something to her, and she said, 'Christina.'

Josico said, 'Stay here tonight.'

'But...'

'No,' he hushed me. He rang Javier. While he dialled the number and waited for Javier to answer the phone, I thought, *I didn't do anything wrong.* Then I heard, 'Javier,' from Josico as he turned away from me. He said, 'Chris is here, mate, and she'll stay with us tonight.' Then they spoke in Spanish. I went upstairs to the bathroom and when I looked at my body in the mirror, there were bruises around my throat and shoulders. I cried – to think I had been treated so badly when I did nothing wrong. I was never unfaithful to Javier. I may have secretly admired two of his brothers and one guy in our street in Hastings Crossing due to my unhappiness. But I'd never done anything to hurt him.

I returned to the lounge room. Josico was sitting, talking to his mother. He said, 'Chris, come and sit with us. It's okay for you to stay here tonight with us.' I thought, *Javier must have agreed to me staying here.* So I sat with them and sobered inwardly. This was the first time I hadn't slept at home with my husband.

The next day, I returned to our house, and of course, Javier was all apologies, like always. I felt the alcohol was having more effect on him and triggering something in his brain.

That Christmas, Javier bought me a gift, which he'd never done before, because I bought my own gifts and preferred it that way. He bought me a clear blue aquamarine ring, which I didn't like. It looked cheap. I could never wear it because I never liked it. Anyway, it was too late; our marriage was ended. We tried to put some life into our marriage by trying to be romantic in the car. But the damage was already done; there were too many unnecessary words told to me too often, over our twenty-two years of marriage. There was only one other time he'd bought me a gift. He'd bought me some carnations, which were my favourite flowers, for my twenty-fifth birthday. I was so happy when I received those flowers. I loved them. But I never received any more.

Chapter 24

My First Granddaughter Is Born

Julian had completed his three years at university at the end of '91, but he wanted to get his degree in nursing, so he and Gerry agreed that he'd do his fourth year, even though they were expecting their first child in February. It was a good opportunity to do it before the free nursing course opportunity ran out.

They were living in the granny flat at the back of Gerry's parents' house. The flat was Gerry's brother Hudson's, but he was away, so they used it. It really was a beautiful flat and contained all they needed. So in the New Year of 1992 they'd settled, and both seemed very happy in their marriage. Julian was getting used to the country life and was learning to ride a horse. His mother-in-law, Gertrude, was amazed at his skills as a horseman, seeing as he'd never ridden a horse in his life. But both his great-grandfather Kinread and my father (his grandfather) were excellent horsemen.

Once a week, Julian was instructing Taekwondo classes in the Spencer Shire Community Hall, as well as doing his fourth year in nursing at the Dawson Hill University. He also had a part-time job in the local

Denver Shire nursing home. He and Gerry were coping, and he seemed to enjoy his new work and his life.

It was on the 8th of February, 1992, that Bonnie-Claire entered the world. Her birth brought me so much joy. I was ecstatic; she was so beautiful. Julian was so proud, and Gerry looked the picture of motherhood. Julian was present throughout the birth, and Gerry had to have a Caesarean section. The night of our granddaughter's birth, I experienced such elation I'd never felt before – which caused Javier and I to have an encounter we'd never experienced in our twenty-two years of marriage.

I didn't know what was happening to me, and neither did Javier. When we made out that night, I had my first orgasm. Javier asked, 'What's up, what's wrong?' I didn't answer him and allowed whatever was happening to me to be carried through. The experience was wonderful, and after it was over I said, as I rolled off the top of him and lay near him, 'I don't know what happened, but I think I orgasmed.'

I was drained from the experience, and lay in the silence of my mind and listened to my heart beating rhythmically to something – that was all part of everything. I don't know what that was, but I was in awe of it. Javier lay near me, and I closed my eyes and gradually fell into a deep sleep. When I awoke the next morning, we didn't talk about what had happened that night, and I didn't want to share my feeling with him, so it remained mine and mine alone.

On and off we'd go out to visit Julian, Gerry and Bonnie-Claire; they were still living in the granny flat. To me, it seemed like my and Javier's life was being played out again: when we lived on the farm for two and a half years before we got our house in Hastings Crossing. We lived with my grandma, mum and dad. Julian was with his mother-in-law, like Javier was with his mother-in-law, my mother. The patterns were being played out. I had to stay with my parents, but my own mother was with her mother-in-law, my father's mother, when they got married. I could see the similarities in our lives. However, for Julian, like us, that wouldn't be permanent. It would take him two and a half years to own his own home, exactly like us, and when he did, his whole life would change. The only difference was that Julian, Javier and I would get to move on. My mother didn't – she ended up living under the control of my father's mother. Hopefully this scenario was going to change.

Julian was an excellent father and husband; many times, Javier and I went out there and Gerry was in bed, sleeping. Julian was doing all the housework and feeding the baby, or he was carrying the baby around in a papoose on his chest while he worked in the house. Julian was like me: he didn't always allow his mother-in-law to take over and care for his child. The child was his to care for.

But later on, Gerry became obsessed with Bonnie-Claire and put the child before Julian. She wouldn't even allow her mother to care for her baby, not even to give her and Julian some time together. Gerry became overly protective and devoted to her child. As time went on, Gerry put all her energies into her child, and gradually forgot about Julian's needs. Julian still loved to go out and he wanted them to enjoy themselves as well as being parents – to go to the movies or for dinner and have time out from their child, but Gerry refused. She made lots of excuses to not leave the child with anyone, even for a minute. There was nothing anyone could do, and it was left for them to sort it out. Julian also couldn't talk to us about it, and he didn't want to bring it up. At the same time, our lives were pretty shaky. We both had our own troubles.

Life was changing for me. I started to make more friends at work, and I was now working as a full-time house manager. The lady who had first trained me on the job became a close friend. Carol insisted that I start a TAFE course in the year 1992. It was a course in aged care that she and Emere were attending. She encouraged me by stating that further studies would help me get a promotion at the Mako facility. She was good at seeing into the future, as far as jobs were concerned. I couldn't imagine myself moving up the scale there. However, Carol's insistence paid off. She convinced me to do the older people's care course. It was a part-time course for two years, and I successfully convinced Javier to let me do it.

I went to TAFE, and as the course went on, I was terrified because I felt I was almost illiterate, even though the course was very basic. I couldn't spell properly or concentrate on what was being said in class. I had learning difficulties and I was having problems keeping up with the lecturers as they spoke. I feared the thought of an exam. Nonetheless, I was so glad Carol had recommended those studies to me, because I had to force myself to write and read again. As time went on, this study caused me some problems at home with Javier. Again, I wasn't going to allow him to stop me.

I got to the point where I didn't care what he thought, especially after what he had done to me after the Christmas party. I felt, too, that he was thinking twice about upsetting me too much. He did calm down a little, because his family knew what was going on in our house, and I think his mother must have spoken to him about it.

So twice weekly, I would go to the Technical College in Fern Hill after work. Stretching my brain was good for me, regardless of nothing coming easy for me. My head was dead, so to say, and everything I was learning was so simple, but it was complex to me. Complex to analyse it and synthesise it. Sometimes I felt daunted by learning. I'd lost all the concepts and skills I needed to learn. It's true, the old saying: 'If you don't use it, you lose it.' In June of that year I also completed an activities course at the request of Ruby, one of the Mako Hostel supervisors.

Chapter 25

Dreams In The Lead-Up
To Leaving Javier

In March 1992, a young man came to work at the facility; he worked in the dementia unit, and his name was Simon. I didn't know why, but I had a big pull towards Simon, and it was so strange of an encounter; I couldn't reason it out or understand why. When I was first introduced to Simon, we both moved back a step, like we both knew something greater than us. It was like I already knew him, I felt from another lifetime. It was an instant recognition on a deeper level. I was becoming more aware of things, but I had no words for what I was experiencing. I knew what it was on a simple level. He and I had encountered a previous life together as souls. We were connected, and I knew we'd agreed to help each other this lifetime, and this was what he did for me.

Since I was a child, I'd always believed in life after death, and that we returned to the earth to re-live another life. I just didn't have the words to express what I meant, which I'd find out later on was reincarnation. As we worked together, I felt a deep love for Simon. I couldn't control these feelings of love for him. I went from a size 12 in my clothes to a size 8 in a matter of a couple of months, and I became more and more in love with him, and it was my secret. I vowed to myself I would never tell a soul, and that no one must know, because he was only 29 and I was 40.

So I loved him from a distance, and he was such a nice person. He made me feel like I could conquer the world, that I was truly a lovely person and worth looking at as a human being.

However, Simon was gay, and when I found this out, it didn't worry me one bit, because my love for him had nothing to do with sexual orientation; this love was on a soul level. The love I felt for him was through the connection of souls, who had each agreed to remind the other of their mission and what they had to do. He was there to remind me of this. The experience was like an inner knowing on my part. Meeting him gave me the strength and energy to carry out my mission.

Having no sexual desire for him was for a greater reason. Nothing would ever develop between us; it would only help me on a soul level. His role was to help me to leave my husband; it was like souls saying, 'Don't forget our arrangement.' It was so hard, secretly loving him, and harder still to keep that secret. I had so many secrets in my life. Life was moving and change was inevitable. There were so many women at work there, and women can pick up on one another. I had to be careful not to let my guard down and expose myself. Furthermore, I never really trusted women at all.

I wanted to know the truth about life. I didn't know who I was and it was time to find this out. I felt that falling in love with Simon had helped me to open up to the spiritual world that I wasn't fully in, or didn't fully understood, due to being so asleep in my marriage; but I knew with him in my life, all was going to change.

I started to have stranger dreams, and as well as dreams, I was having visions. I would go to bed at night-time, and just before going off to sleep, while lying in the bed, these visions came. In these visions, I was travelling through the universe. I was flying at a fast speed through space. It was like a movie I was watching from another part of me, but not from my two physical eyes. I was fully awake, going through a kaleidoscope of colour, a spiralling of colours. It was like I was in an invisible flying aircraft, going through space. I wasn't afraid, but I never went anywhere; just there, up into the universe, and then I'd fall into a deep, deep sleep, and as I slept, I felt like I'd died through the night. At this time of my life, I had no idea what was happening to me, because I had no knowledge of spiritual experiences; there was no one to talk to about these experiences.

I had slept deeply all my life and I used to ask to Javier to wake me if the house caught fire, because I'd never wake. He would sometimes ask me the next morning if I heard such-and-such noises in the street; I never did. And many times in our earlier days, when the boys went out for the night, he'd wait up for them to return home; not me. I knew they'd return safely. But he never trusted that they would. Once, Julian got put in the lock-up for defending his friend in a fight. Unfortunately, he ended up in trouble. But it was okay;

Javier had gotten a call and woke me, and we went to the station and dealt with it.

The people I worked with didn't ever speak on a spiritual level, and back then I didn't even know of the word 'spiritual' and what it implied. I somehow knew I was travelling through the eye of my Essence, and my Essence was trying to convey to me the universe and its glory and its oneness. I was being awakened from my long sleep.

Dreams were becoming so real, and I wanted to question life more and more to find out why things were as they were. Crocodiles and dinosaurs kept entering my night-world and I knew both were connecting to me to remember ancient things, because these creatures, I would learn, were ancient reptiles. But I had too many emotional issues to be dealt with, and it would still take a while before I could move in that spiritual direction.

How confined I was. So much so that I wasn't living my life to its fullest potential, or expressing or living in my truth.

Working with the elderly was a great time for me. They were teaching me many things about life and people's behaviour that I never comprehended; it would be a ten-year learning period there. I would say Mako was a learning field, and it was. I was learning about different people, personalities, and behaviours, and most importantly I was learning how to deal with these personalities and behaviours. And through all this I was discovering who I was, through other people. I could see things in them that were in me. This puzzled me.

There were so many different aspects of me bottled up within. Unbeknown to us, we carry so much that isn't ours, but the result of learning from our role models, families, and peers. Also, it is what we bring in from previous lifetimes, and what we bring back with us to work through that we never completed in those previous lifetimes.

I was blindly seeking myself through an inner knowing that knew better than me. It was my intuition, I was told, and when I first heard that word I thought, What was that? So the journey began.

At this time, I was learning about psychics from my work friends. They told me about places I could go to learn about my future; this intrigued me. I was very curious, and I went to get a reading from these ladies.

There was one lady called Naomi, who lived in Wentworth, and she kept telling me that I was gold. She said, 'Chris, you are gold, but you don't know it yet, and you have a big future ahead of you. And you will achieve many things and guide and help others. You're special, and don't let anyone tell you any differently.'

'But how, Naomi?' I'd ask her.

She said, 'It will all unfold in time.' But her words left me puzzled, and she advised me, 'Don't push it, let it flow in its time.' I thought, *I'm special* and *Let it flow* – what does it all mean? I had no idea how I could possibly help other people or be special, because I was stuck in my marriage, and had no academic education because I left school in Year Four as we called it in my days. I was seventeen. I had no career behind me, and I was almost illiterate, except for this TAFE course I was doing. It was helping me to get my mind slowly working again.

I thought, *How can I help other people?* I can hardly help myself. Oddly enough, Naomi told me that I was here to help my mother organise and manage her life; she told me that my mother and I had a past life together in Malaysia. Well, I could understand that. I was here to help Mum organise her life. I agreed with her on that. She told me that when I had property and money, I must put it into my boys' names, so it wouldn't be stolen from me. Now, that was confusing; I couldn't see myself having money or property.

My mind constantly questioned things Naomi told me, and I pondered on life and where I was at. Naomi's words kept echoing through my head: 'It will all unfold as it's supposed to.' But I wasn't looking for these messages. I wanted answers, not riddles. I also wanted answers in regard to my husband and me. Where were we going in our marriage? However, there were no solutions for us, and Naomi never said anything about him. She told me that I'd meet other men in later life. I guessed from that that we'd probably split up.

In regard to my mum, I told Naomi I'd been caring for her all my life, and that I'd been her confidant since I was a very young child. I was the only one who'd ever listened to her troubles.

But Naomi told me, 'No, this will be different. You and she have shared many past lives together.' That, I agreed with. I felt we did share many past lifetimes together. I told Naomi about my father and how we had some things between us that may be considered not right, not disclosing too much of my secret. But she insisted that it was my mum and I who were mostly connected. She puzzled me more and more.

To get answers, I'd go to various readers. On one of my visits to a lady in Eddington, Javier followed me out there, but I didn't know he had followed me. I was so depressed that I didn't see his car behind me. I had no idea how he found out I was going to these psychic readers. After my reading, when I was leaving the lady's house and walking to her front gate, I glimpsed Javier in Jerod's car.

Terror seized me, and I just pretended I didn't see him. I got into my car and drove off. He didn't mention the event to me that night. But the next day, the lady called me, and she told me my husband had come to her front door and asked her why I'd gone to her house. I never asked her what he said. This lady had told me I'd never leave Javier, but deep down I knew I had to, to complete my life and do something I wasn't yet aware of.

Javier and I had a hard time in our marriage; it was failing more and more every day. Kay seemed to be concerned for my well-being. I began to trust her and decided to confide in her about my feelings towards Simon. I felt I could tell her because Simon had been dismissed from work, and no one knew why. It was a big announcement: he was gone.

It wasn't as if I was troubled by Simon, because he'd left work. However, I missed his presence around the facility, and he still had a hold on my heart. I heard that Violet, the new activities officer in the dementia unit, was behind him being sacked. I was told by some people to be careful of her, because she had two faces.

Nonetheless, I didn't understand why she'd have Simon sacked, because they were very friendly. Anyway, he'd come in to do what he had to do: to help me on a spiritual level, and that was it. I guess he had to go. But the love had pulled at my heart, and it was so intense. To be honest, my pain was very intense, in regard to my love for him.

Silly me; I'd made a big mistake with Kay, because she'd called our house when I wasn't home and talked to Javier. Kay had told Javier about my infatuation with a young man at the facility.

Well, Javier saw red. He called Julian to the house when Jerod was home, on the day he decided to confront me about Simon. He screamed at me and told me that he knew about my boyfriend from work, and that Kay had told him when she'd rung the house.

I was stunned for a moment. Again, I was betrayed by a woman. Javier had a field day, calling me all the names he could think of in front of our two sons, and all I could do was tell him that it wasn't true; there was no boyfriend and it wasn't what he thought it was.

There was no reasoning with Javier – I was a prostitute and a slut. I didn't fight back. I looked at the boys, and they were also quiet and just listened. I said, 'Javier, I felt for this person, but he never knew it, it was only on my part; the person had no idea I liked him.' I was so upset with Kay, more than with Javier. I had trusted her, and I thought, *How come she was talking to Javier? And why did she do this?*

Javier was inconsolable and wouldn't listen to reason. He went on and on and over it to make his point. Our marriage was at its end, and I couldn't fight.

That day I just looked at the boys, and they turned their eyes down and walked off. I was alone. Couldn't they see what I was faced with? Couldn't they see I'd lost all love for their father and it was dead? But they couldn't see it. Julian went home and Jerod didn't speak to me that night.

At work the following day, I confronted Kay about the incident. She told me she had not said anything to damage my marriage; she'd told him I was friends with many people at work. She told me Javier had asked her if there were any men at work. She told him that there was a young man called Simon, but he'd left. She played innocent. After hearing her version of the story, I said, 'You told Javier I was interested in him.'

'No, Chris, I didn't,' she promised.

I searched her face, but she was busying herself. I stated, 'I told you I liked him as I like everyone.' She dismissed it as a Mediterranean man's jealousy of his woman, which I had no idea about. From then on, I didn't know who to trust, but I had to give Kay the benefit of the doubt. I would eventually leave Javier. Simon was there to spur me on; even though he'd gone, his spirit was still connecting with mine, to remind me to take courage and to find my own inner strengths.

However, that didn't free me; I went straight back into hell.

Chapter 26

Messages From Beyond

The mood in the household was bad; there was a big breakdown in our marriage, and many more fights between us, or there was complete silence. I remember coming home from work tired and exhausted – from my life, not the job.

I rarely drank a lot of water. I was mainly a coffee drinker, but one day I was compelled to get a glass of water. As I rested my body against the bench, I felt pensive. As I drank the water, I felt someone accidentally bump into me. Automatically, I said, 'Oh, sorry.' Realising I was alone in the house, I looked around and there was no one, only me. I felt it was my nephew, Alex.

I wasn't afraid of the presence. I felt protected by him. When Chantal came home that day, before the others arrived home, I asked her, 'Chantal, do you feel a presence in this house?'

She stood very close to me and looked at me. She said, with wide open eyes looking around as if searching the house, 'Yes, there is, Chris.'

'Hmm, I felt it today. I think it's my nephew, Alex. I felt he'd come in to help me.' She nodded and moved in as closely as she could to me. I looked at her and said, 'But don't tell Jerod, he'll freak out.'

As if she knew, she said, 'I know, he hates to talk about things like that.'

I said, 'Yeah, I know, but he tells me he has had out-of-body experiences, and he still denies the other side of life.' I paused as I put the jug on for coffee, and said, 'But Jerod is so scared of the unknown, and I understand that fear. I too was once like that when I was younger, and only recently I've started to understand the unknown and learn not be afraid of it.'

As the days progressed, more strange things happened in the house. I knew it was from the other side, and that they were backing me up and supporting me. I'd come home from work and through the back door on a particular day. Javier was sitting on the sofa in the family room, watching TV. He said something nasty to me as I walked alongside the kitchen cabinet that housed the kitchen sink on the upper level. As I neared the step to step up onto that next level, I was about to react to his comment when the TV flickered wildly and made a static buzzing noise.

With one foot on the step, I lowered it down and stopped. I knew I was being warned to let it go. I stepped back onto the step and walked off, knowing I was protected, and feeling safe in this protection.

It was getting closer to when I would really experience an amazing spiritual event – one to put me into a new beginning, a new life, a new self: a stronger, more confident and courageous self.

I was forty-one years old and couldn't bear this life. I'd searched myself and couldn't find the answers I wanted. I'd tried the books, and they were not fulfilling me enough. I needed to leave this marriage. I felt like a prostitute. Having sex with Javier made me want to put my hand out for a payment. If I could've, I'd have told him to leave fifty dollars on the table. All that was holding me together was my job. I was so glad I had a decent job. On a deeper level, I knew I had many lessons to learn around my issues with age, oldness, sickness, deception and jealousy. My work there at Mako had opened me up to all these realisations for me to look at myself. But I was not affected by it – or was I? I was not in alignment with what was happening.

In my childhood, Mum and Grandma had some harrowing times. They were jealous and had jealousies between themselves. But it never affected me. My sister was jealous, but I didn't feel jealous towards her. These emotions were all unknown to me; I didn't know this was part of the quest to find out who I was. The journey had begun since birth; however, there were too many interruptions, so I wasn't aware of a journey.

Nonetheless, my fortieth birthday showed me how alone I was. There was no party for me, because I couldn't invite friends. Javier had too much control over my life. I couldn't breathe without his permission.

Then came the night my life changed.

We were home alone, Javier and me. Jerod was at Chantal's house. I don't know how it all started; however, there was a big fight between us. It was so big that I was near to unconsciousness. My mind went blank; it had blanked out on me. I didn't know who I was, or where I was, in this state.

I collapsed and fell to the floor of the lounge room, where the fight was taking place. Seeing me in this collapsed state, Javier became frightened. He realised he'd pushed me too far. I could barely remember him carrying me to our bedroom and putting me on our bed. I heard him calling my name from a distance. He sat me up on the edge of the bed and called to me, 'Chrissy, Chrissy.' I was half in and out. I was saying, 'Who am I, I don't know where I am, what's going on? Who am I?' I truly lost myself.

He held my arms and opened the bed sheets and placed me into the bed and pulled the covers over me, then he got into the bed beside me. We lay there, and I started to regain my senses, but I was dazed. Then out of the blue I sat up erect. I looked at Javier, and I saw his eyes bulging out of his head. He had drawn the sheet up to his eyes. I felt something in the room; it was strong and powerful. I became fully conscious and turned to Javier and said, 'A presence has just walked into this room, and it's come in to help me, or it's a stronger side of me entering me.'

They were my last words. I lay down and closed my eyes and fell into a deep, deep sleep. I don't know what Javier did, but I'd left him with the sheet around his eyes, staring out from behind it, terrified, the light still on.

The following morning, I woke as if nothing had happened. He never talked about it, but I knew then I was safe. My strength grew and I was able to get on with my life and make changes to leave this man.

That was the opening, and after that night, I said to Javier, 'I want to start to look for a house, because I'm going to leave you.'

He looked at me and said, 'We can work it out.'

I said, 'But I still want to look at houses. Let's see what happens.' I felt stronger after that event in the bedroom, and I knew it was time to leave.

Javier and I went house-hunting to many places. He took me to some real dumps, and there were places where the whole inside of the house needed to be redone. He knew I couldn't live like that, that I had a standard, and there was no way I could buy a house and repair it on my own.

He'd take me to old Commission house areas where the houses were being sold to private owners. But this wasn't for me – I knew I could do better.

Around this time, it was Julian and Gerry's first wedding anniversary. I found out that they were having their own issues. Julian had told me he had asked Gerry to leave their baby, Bonnie-Claire, with her mother so they could celebrate their wedding anniversary. Apparently, Gerry refused to leave the baby with her mother. This upset Julian, because he wanted to spend their anniversary together. He told me that after some coaxing, he'd convinced her to go out. So they got dressed up, and he was so happy, he told me, until they got down the road, and about ten minutes from the house Gerry cried and complained and virtually begged him to take her home again. He gave in to her and they returned home to the baby and never went out.

This concerned me. I asked him if he'd talked to Gertrude, his mother-in-law, about it, but he felt she wouldn't listen to him. Gerry was in constant fear of her baby being left with others. She was reminding me of me, and how I'd never let anyone tend to Julian or Jerod when they were babies. However, Gertrude was a safe and good person, and I couldn't understand Gerry's behaviour.

Chapter 27

Solicitors

Disillusionment and hurt crept more and more into our lives, and I was wanting out. So Javier and I went to our solicitor, Vince. I'd agreed that we would both use the same solicitor. I didn't want to drag our case through a divorce court, because all of that could become a drawn-out process and take years – also, that method could work out too expensive. Nonetheless, I remembered on one of our visits to their office, Vince and his partner, Mitchell, both asked me, 'Christine, are you sure you're happy with the settlement of sixty-one thousand and the family car Javier is offering you?'

I never hesitated. I said, 'Yes, I am, Vince.' In my mind, I wasn't, but I couldn't stay with him any longer, and I knew he was getting out of our settlement cheaply.

'You can go further and take him to court and get more money,' I heard Vince imply. I looked at Javier, who sat alongside the solicitors and I was sitting out in front of them, as if at a distance from these three men. I was out on my own, and it felt like I didn't fit into this scene being played out between the four of us.

Answering Vince in an almost subdued voice, I said, 'No, I've had enough, and I want out as quickly as possible.'

As if Vince knew I had to go, he stated, 'Okay, but you must remember, too, Christine…' He paused as he looked over at Javier, then said, 'You have two years to change your mind, and you can take Javier to court to get extra money.'

Half-interested, I nodded and said, 'Okay, I will remember that.'

I knew Javier was getting away with murder, so to say, and I was getting less money than I should. However, my sanity was more important. There was one thing I'd never touch, and that was his superannuation, because to me that was his.

Life was getting more difficult in the house, and we seemed to be fighting more often. In my mind, I wasn't happy with the settlement; maybe Vince was right, and I should be going for extra money. One afternoon when Javier returned from work, I decided to take a chance and ask him for extra money. I heard him arrive home and open the garage door. A little while later, I heard him drive the car into the garage and switch the engine off. I took a breath and questioned in my mind: *Should I or shouldn't I ask him for extra money?* I could hear him coming around the path to the back door of the house. I felt tense and scared all in one feeling. Would I chance it? Was it worth it? It was just an extra ten thousand I was asking for. But I knew what he was like when it came to giving up his money. I stood in the family room near the step that led up into the kitchen area and waited for him.

He entered the house, saw me standing there, and looked away from me. I'd blocked the way to the steps. He stopped and sensed I had a question. 'What's wrong with you?' he asked.

Bracing myself, I said, 'Javier, I need to talk to you.' He immediately shifted his eyes to me and glared at me, questioning me as if to say, *What about?* It was as if we both stopped, then I said bravely, 'Javier, I want to ask you for an extra ten thousand dollars in my settlement.'

As if attacking like a bandit from behind a bush, he pounced on me. I felt myself being pushed up against the sofa's arm and the wall. I said, 'Javier, I want that extra money and I will ask the lawyers for it.'

A monster seemed to have entered him, and his facial expressions became deranged; his eyes glowed with hatred for me. I gulped, thinking, *What have I done?* He grabbed my throat with both his hands and pressed into the flesh of my neck. In shock, I said, 'Ow, Javier, don't do that.' I tried to release his grip with my hands, but he had me in a strangle hold and his grip was too tight around my throat. Then, without warning, he threw me by my throat flat on my back onto the sofa cushions. I landed, winding myself, and the jolt hurt my back. I couldn't move, and I didn't know which was the worst pain: the pain in my neck from him squeezing it, or my back, or my pride. I tried to slowly sit up, and gradually brought my legs around to the floor. When I sat up, I held my back, and Javier just glared at me.

He backed off, looking at me with contempt, and warned me, 'If you ask for any more money, I will have you killed. I can arrange it.' That was all the concern I got from him, and again he'd shown me his deranged side and his love of money.

I looked at him as I stroked my throat gently with my fingers; the tightness of his grip had caused me to begin to cough, and the pain in my back was great. I knew I just had to get out of this house and be content with what I could get from him. I knew I could manage with what I would get. Javier walked off and I lay down on the sofa and let my body rest from the stress I'd encountered. I felt both physically and emotionally drained, and I knew his threats weren't idle; he could arrange my death. He wouldn't need to go any further than his brother John, because of John's involvement with the Mafia years ago.

Thoughts of Gema surfaced. She'd told me how, in a bad temper, John shot one of their cats. He never warned anyone, just got a pistol out of the boot of the car and shot it, all because it was on his new Mustang. Again, I slowly sat up and sighed, resolving within me that I just wanted out of this marriage.

After that incident, I had to quickly find a house. We'd go house-hunting periodically. He'd always go with me; I guess he wanted to control me right up until I left him. Javier had it in his mind that if by some miracle we got back together; we could use the house I bought as an investment. That was his idea – far from my idea, because I was not going to stay with him. I had outgrown him, and I was slowly dying a death of stagnation.

However, miracles did happen for me: I found my home alone, without his assistance or interference.

It was a Sunday afternoon when this opportunity came my way. Javier and I had been house-hunting and I was truly disillusioned by this stage, thinking I would never find a decent home for myself that I liked. We'd just returned to our home, and of course, we had been arguing on the way. Normally, I'd just go into the house and up into our bedroom and sulk and come back out an hour or so later, when things calmed down. However, not this day. I drove into the driveway, and while Javier opened the garage door, I drove back up out of the driveway and off up our street onto the main road. This time, I headed to Claire Point Beach.

At the beach front on the hill on the main road, I parked the car, overlooking the ocean, and said to myself, 'This is where I want to live.' Sitting there, I relaxed and stared at the ocean and wondered, *How can I do that? I can't afford a house in this area, not with the money I'm getting from the settlement.*

I stepped out of the car and stood, leaning on the open car door. The waves rolled in on the beach and there was something soothing when they crashed on the shoreline. Out in the sea, there were many surfers who rode these beautiful waves to shore. Beach goers were basking in the sun. How I loved the sea and its mightiness; but feared its depths and what lay below it. I stretched and breathed in the clean sea air. I wasn't the only one enjoying the view. Others had parked their cars to collect their thoughts and admire the beauty of the sea.

I re-entered my car, sat, and closed the door, leaning my chin on my hands as I embraced the steering wheel. I stared out the window, not thinking; I was just absorbing nature. I backed away from the steering wheel and thought, *I'd better get home.* I turned on the ignition and checked the road – it was all clear. I backed out of the parking space and drove down the street. I passed the house that Brook lived in many years ago. He was a past love I had after leaving school. I thought back to those years and marvelled at how I still remembered where his mother's house was. I never guessed I'd end up living where we'd first met. Claire Point Beach was just a ten-minute drive from my own house.

As I drove, I remembered how Brook had said to me, 'I'll never marry a virgin, Chris.' I smiled to myself and wondered what ever happened to him. Strange, though; Dad and Mum told me they'd met a great guy on the North Coast when they were holidaying there. Dad said his name was Brook, and he used to live at Claire Point. When Dad told me that, I turned quickly to him and asked, 'At Claire Point?'

'Yes, he lived there with his mother and left there years ago, and travelled.'

'Dad…' I said, surprised. 'I wonder if that was the Brook I knew when I was seventeen?' Of course, Dad didn't know. The world was a small place, and if it was, well, there was nothing I could do about it. I'd made my bed with Javier. How much had I given up for him? Mostly my freedom. I'd also burned all my love letters from Brook and other boys who had admired me. Now I realised how silly I was to let Javier frighten me.

Before I knew it, I was on Rose Tree Road, a road I'd never used before. I'd lost myself in my thoughts and memories and forgotten what I was doing. Then I realised where I was. As I approached the street before the roundabout, I slowed down, and to my right I saw a house for sale; it was a private sale, and it didn't have a real estate agent's sign. I pulled over onto the side of the road, stopped the car, and wrote down the phone number displayed on the For Sale sign. I decided to call the owner on Monday. It was Sunday, and we were raised to not call in on people unannounced on a Sunday.

I was so excited, as if I had inside knowledge that I had found my house. I never told Javier on my return to our house. He did ask me, 'Where did you go?'

I calmly said, 'To the beach, I needed some fresh air.' He didn't question me any more on the topic; we didn't speak for the rest of the night.

Monday came, and after work I went to that house on Rose Tree Road. I was excited and nervous, and hoped I could afford the house. I went to the front door and knocked; there was no answer. On my right was another door, so I knocked on it. Shortly, I was greeted by a man.

Nervously, I said, 'I'm here about your house – I saw a For Sale sign.'

'Come in,' he said, and he walked off as he called out to his wife. I stood and waited in their lounge room. I looked around the front room and thought, *This is my house.*

Next, the man was being followed by a woman. He said, 'This is my wife, Iris, and my name's Morton.'

'Hi, my name's Chris.' I explained how on Sunday I had driven past their house and saw the sign, but I didn't want to call in. He reassured me I could have. But I shrugged and smiled. Then he showed me the house. I knew this was my house. Morton and his wife had to move into a retirement village at Garlands. He told me this was due to him having little strokes; he needed to make sure his wife wasn't left burdened with their big house. I could see that he'd had a major stroke somewhere in his life. He then explained that he'd had one when he was forty.

The house was a great buy, with a swimming pool out the back. It was just wonderful, and had a granny flat as well. The other door I'd first knocked on had a permanent boarder, who had been with them for some time. The house was like a rabbit warren, with many outlets here and there. This side of the house was where Morton and Iris lived. It had one bedroom with an enormous sitting room and a built-in wardrobe off the bathroom. There were extra plusses: they were leaving all their furniture behind. Oh, my goodness me, all my dreams had come true at once. I hadn't thought of buying furniture. With their furniture I wouldn't have to.

Morton was really friendly, and explained how he was buying the retirement unit from Victoria and Peter who'll move to Mako Hostel.

'No?' I said.

Surprised by my reaction, he said, 'Yes, Victoria and Peter.'

You could have knocked me over with a feather. I said, 'Guess what?'

'What?' he asked.

'Well, I work at Mako Hostel as a cook – I'm working in Primrose Cottage and those two people are the two new residents who are coming in to be cared for.'

'Well, I never,' he said.

I said, 'Yes, it's all meant to be, and how small is the world?'

I realised this more and more – how connected we were. Somehow, I knew I was supposed to connect to these people, who were connected to Victoria and Peter. How strange. I worked in a retirement hostel and the house I worked and cooked in was where the couple was going to live after Iris and Morton bought their unit in Garlands. I realised it was all about connections.

As I listened, I felt it was like a dream. But it wasn't; it was all real. I would be taking care of Victoria and Peter, and I would buy Morton and Iris' house. I was all smiles, and I didn't know why, but I thought, *I have to take care of Victoria and Peter to be able to get the house from Morton and Iris.* It was like an unconscious agreement between us all.

My whole life shifted in that house there and then. I would be able to move. I explained to Morton that I now had to go to a bank and find the finance for the house. He wanted one hundred and forty-one thousand for the property and the furniture, which included a Chesterfield lounge setting. Morton told me that he had another lady interested in the house, a school teacher, and if I wanted the house, I'd better hurry and find out if I could get the finance for it.

Chapter 28

Finding The Finances

I had a big job ahead of me. I rang the bank I had banked with from my school days and that we used for our banking in my married life. I hoped that being a long-term customer and having a good credit rating would help me. I made an appointment with the bank manager. On the day of my appointment, talking to a loans officer, I was told I was unable to get a loan. But that didn't faze me. I decided to try another bank, which was advertising home loans to low-income workers. Again, another disappointment: because I'd be paying off the loan as a single woman, I wasn't eligible. Nonetheless, never say die. So I rang up the Premier Bank in Havertown and made an appointment with the manager at that bank.

On the day of my appointment, I went for my interview wearing the tracksuit I had been wearing all day at work, because there was no time to go home and change. I'd had a very busy, terrible day at work, and I felt washed out. I looked sloppy, because I had some food stains on my clothes from cooking fatty food.

I reached the bank at 4pm and was told to sit and wait, so I did. As I waited to be called in, I tried to lower my stress. Then I was called in by a young woman who ushered me into the manager's office. On entering, I saw a kind-faced man in his forties.

He stood up as I entered the room and introduced himself by stating his name, which was Mitchell. I introduced myself in return. He asked me, 'How can I help you?', as he indicated for me to sit. I sat forward in my chair so as to be closer to him to get my message across. I told him I needed a loan for a home of my own because I was divorcing my husband, and that I had found this wonderful house, and it had a boarder to help me to pay the loan off, should I be able to get one. I told him I was getting sixty-one thousand from my husband when I decided to buy a house. Mitchell never said a word; he just studied me. When I stopped talking, he said without hesitation, 'You've got the loan.'

Shocked, I sat back in my chair from leaning forward after explaining my case to him and said, 'I got the loan.'

'Yes.' He nodded, his hands leaning on the arms of his chair, and continued, 'I'm giving you the loan because I can see that you are a determined person and you will do whatever you say you'll do, and you will pay the money back, and no one will stop you in your endeavours.'

I was amazed and dumbfounded that he trusted me and happy all in one, and said, 'Thank you so much.'

He said, 'Now you can fill in these forms and make your application and work it out with your solicitor about your settlement, and then we can proceed from there.'

So I filled in the required forms and thanked him again and left. I felt elated, happy, and amazed that that person saw so much in me.

Later, on one of our trips to the shopping centre, I was coming up the escalator with Javier behind me, and there was the bank manager at the top of the escalator. I introduced him to Javier. He looked at me as if to say, *I understand why you're leaving him.* That look helped me and my determination to succeed in paying off my loan and starting a new life. I was doing the right thing.

Everything started to fall in line. I got my settlement and the loan from the Premier Bank, and my house. Morton and Iris moved into Garlands, and Victoria and Peter moved into Primrose Cottage and I told them how I was the person who'd bought Morton and Iris' house, and I was so happy. They were also amazed at the coincidence of coming to Mako Hostel and actually being looked after by the person who'd bought the house off the people who'd bought their unit at Garlands.

I was in the right place at the right time to join in on this connection between the five of us. Morton, Iris, Victoria, Peter, and me. And better still, I found a house I truly liked that was close to Claire Point Beach, which was just five minutes away. So I got to go to where I wanted to be.

It was the 23rd of October, 1992, and I couldn't stand this anymore. I was in an indecisive mood as usual. I was forty-one years old; Javier and I had been together for almost twenty-two years. I'd wanted to wait until Jerod had finished his university in February, because I'd always told Javier that when the boys were educated,

I'd leave him. Things had changed and I had to make a decision. Did I hold on to that promise or go? I couldn't bear it anymore. On the day I made the decision, my parents were at the house. It was a good opportunity to move, because there'd be less fighting, and they could help me to move. I thought to myself, *How much does one have to take in their life?* I had to break that promise to Jerod and go.

I was tired of living a lie; I was dead and void. I thought Jerod could manage for the last leg of his studies, but I was in two minds, so I asked Jerod if he minded if I moved out that day while Nana and Pop were there. He said, 'Mum, if you're not happy here, go.' Jerod saw the pain I was in. Javier had been asking me to stay just a little longer, but I couldn't. I felt encouraged by Jerod's words and thought, *I'm going; why should I stay here, when I have a house to move into where I could have peace of mind?* Also, my parents were here. The time was right; I had help and it would be easier to leave. The five of us in this selling-and-purchasing venture had decided to move at the same time, and it was as if each of us was helping the other to move on. So not long after the four moved, I moved into my home.

I announced to Javier, 'I've decided to move out today while my mum and dad are here, and they can help me with the moving.'

Shocked and unable to react in front of my parents, he said, 'Well, go, if that's what you want.' He looked at my parents and he was stuck; he couldn't retaliate or hit me or grab my throat. He had to let me go this time without a fight, because he'd never show the audience his true self – he had an image to uphold.

Next, I pulled my clothes from the wardrobe and I took my unicorn. That was all I took. And that was all he'd allow me to take from the ornaments or other possessions we'd collected over the years. He acted sweetly in front of my parents, telling me that the other ornaments were always here, and that I could collect them later on and we could talk about them. But to me they weren't important. We put my things in our cars, and we transported them to my new home.

During the couple of trips from my old home to my new home, Javier asked me to reconsider, and to change my mind and stay. I said, 'No, Javier, I can't, I've had enough; I have to go.' Before, I'd wanted the boys to be educated, but I also felt sorry for him, and that was another reason why I'd stayed for so long. But I didn't allow my sympathy for him to overrule my sanity. So I left him, even though I could see his sadness. But I felt my freedom more. So that day I left Javier; enough was enough. So what, that we didn't make it to twenty-two years of marriage? There was a new journey waiting for me.

The house we'd shared was big, and suddenly, with my few things gone, it seemed bare and unlived in, as I walked through it for the last time. There seemed to be a loneliness there that swallowed you up. However, I was free at long last from the grip of imprisonment and grief. I could once again breathe. So I walked out of Javier's life.

On my first day away from Javier, I took out the diary that Emere had given me and I made my first entry, and that was the start of me writing in a diary again, after all those years; and I was so happy to write again.

Chapter 29

Inner Guilt

I didn't know why, but Jerod decided to come and live with me; but in a way I knew why deep down, because he was the meat in the sandwich between his father and me. After I left Javier, I had no interest in him at all, or in whatever he did. His life was now his to do as he pleased. Unfortunately, Javier didn't think likewise, and he wanted to know my ins and outs. Jerod would be his connection for that information, and that would come at a price for Jerod. He would have to live in a terrible hovel in the granny flat at the back of my new home, because I couldn't do it up; I didn't have enough money to repair it. I had to watch my money, and in the builder's report, the flat next door showed damage in the kitchen and bathroom; these issues had to be dealt with first, because it was structural damage to the building.

Jerod only slept in the granny flat, and he used the kitchen in the main section of the house and watched TV with me. I agonised over him being in that horrible flat, when he had a perfectly comfortable home with his father. But many, many years later, I reasoned that Jerod had the choice to go and live with his father, and he didn't. My guilt was immense, but it was his choice, not mine. And back then I often wondered if he was there to scout for his father, and of course he was.

The boys always favoured their dad because they didn't fully understand me, bless their hearts; even though we'd formed a strong bond as they got older, they still always went over to their father's side.

My guilt kept attacking me about the state of the granny flat and the conditions Jerod had to live in. I wanted him to have a comfortable house with everything he needed a good, warm bed, not an old mattress on a boxed bed in a hovel that was cold, old, and inappropriate. I knew he was there to inform his dad. Also, I think he hated to live with his dad, because when I thought about it, Javier would be endlessly going on to Jerod about me leaving him.

So there were many reasons behind his actions. Jerod said he was there to look after me, but I didn't need Jerod's protection. I was a strong woman and I was discovering that. I could see I had changed in the few days I'd left Javier. I'd lost a lot of my fears. For the first time in my life, I could go out in the dark at night-time. I was up until one or two in the morning, cleaning my new house. I just enjoyed my house and the freedom of being alone, and for the first time ever, I could sleep in a totally blackened room with the shades down to block out all light entering the room. I could never do that before. I wasn't running and jumping into bed in fear of my ankles being grabbed – all those fears were gone. I welcomed the dark and loved it. I was losing the old me and her physical and mental fears. I slept so soundly, more soundly than I ever had in my life. I'd always been a deep sleeper; however, I was going deeper into sleep. On waking, I'd jump out of bed immediately, like life was renewed within me.

Chapter 30

The Boarder

Sam was the boarder next door. It was so good to have this split house, and the extra income would be a blessing; although I agonised over declaring it on my tax return, because I was told not to. I needed this money to help me pay my mortgage. I hadn't met Sam yet, because each time I went to the house, I never saw him – even on my first few days in the house, because I was always busy cleaning it and sorting out my stuff. I just enjoyed the house.

It was a few days after I'd moved in. One morning, on returning from the corner shop after buying milk, I saw Sam coming out of the front yard. As I neared the house I said, 'Hi, Sam, how are you?'

I was all smiles and he was grouchy. He looked at me and said, 'I'm good.'

'My name's Chris,' I said.

He growled and said, 'Okay.'

I smiled. 'I hope we can be friends, and I'm sure you're a nice person.'

He looked at me and said, 'I'm not a nice person,' in a harsh voice.

I smiled, saying, 'I think you are.' And I left him and went into my yard and into the house. It wasn't easy between Sam and me at first, but we got to understanding each other over time.

I didn't understand a lot about myself, and never knew who I was, but now I was blessed with a new lease on life. It was three weeks into being in my new house and I decided it was time to travel to get to know myself.

My girlfriend Peggy had moved to Dolphin Point in the north, so I called her. 'Peggy, it's Chris.'

'Princess,' she said. Princess was my pet name from her. When she was younger, she was called Sticks because she was so skinny. Then she became fat, and we'd laugh about that. I told her Dad used to call me Princess, and that's how it all started. Her happiness was oozing out of the phone; Peggy was always so happy-natured.

'I'm going to take three weeks off work. Can I come and stay at your place?'

'Of course, come, and I can't wait to see you.' She was very happy about my proposal, and in the background, I could hear her little boy jumping and laughing as if he knew me, and he was just as excited. So it was decided that I'd go up there. I told her I would be driving up and would be there within a week or so. She said, 'You just come, and I'll be waiting for you.'

I'd never travelled alone before, always with my parents or Javier and the boys. I needed to do this to prove to myself I was capable of doing anything in this world. The return trip I chose to do covered a distance of about two thousand, six hundred and twenty kilometres, and the idea of travelling alone really excited me. I was being challenged by me.

Of course, I let my parents know. Dad checked out my car and gave it a small service and made sure the tyres were in good order and that the spare tyre was usable, but these things didn't seem to worry me or stop me from doing the things I must do. These were minor issues.

The day arrived to go. It was very early in the morning, about 3am, and I wanted to leave by 4am because that was a good time to travel, to have the road to myself. I casually prepared for the day, eating breakfast and putting my last lot of toiletries into my car. While out there, I thought, *Wow, what a wonderful day.* The air was so still in the early hours of the morning, and there was no traffic to be seen. It felt like I was all alone, but this aloneness was a welcome aloneness. I turned and looked at my house and smiled at my achievements. I was so grateful for this house and to the bank manager; I was lucky. I couldn't believe I got that loan, but I did.

Was it meant to be? I wondered, *Do we have a planned destiny?* Somehow it was all meant to happen this way. I leaned on the car door, rested my head on my folded arms on the roof, and looked at my new home. I thought of how, when Javier and I were out shopping and we ran into the bank manager and I introduced Javier to him, I felt Mitchell there and then understanding why I had to leave Javier. I seemed to be able to read his face.

With all my gear in the car, it was time to make sure everything was switched off in the house and everything was in order before I left, because Jerod had decided to stay with his father while I was away. I checked the power points and that everything was unplugged, all the taps were securely off, and the oven was off – all was safe and secure. Then I walked up the long hallway to the front door of my house, which was open. I opened the screen door and stepped out onto the front verandah. As I held the flyscreen door open, I stepped back into the house with one leg to grab the front door to draw it closed. I stopped, and again I looked down the hallway. I wasn't sure why, but I said to the house, for reasons unknown to me 'Goodbye, house.'

Then from nowhere came this surge of energy, flying up the hallway, right up to me, and I calmly said, 'Don't worry, I'll be back in three weeks.'

The energy then subsided. I closed the door, not afraid or bothered about it, and shrugged my shoulders and left. I knew the house was safe and protected.

Chapter 31

Inner Strength

My trip was one of self-realisation that I was a very capable person and had no fears of being on my own and driving for miles. I travelled through towns and cities on the way up to the north of Australia, and stopped off at my friend Lucy's house in Port Foxdale, because I had arranged to call in and spend a few days with her. My stay with Lucy and her husband Randall was wonderful, and they wanted me to stay longer, but I had to move on. I told them I'd call in on my way back if I had time.

My next stop-off point was Carter's Bay; I'd always wanted to go there, and it was a lovely laidback area, but I didn't see too many hippies. I went on a day tour, and on this tour, we were taken out through an amazing area to a place that collected crystals and artefacts. I saw giant amethysts and they were truly amazing. We were allowed to step inside one of these amethysts. I could have stayed in there forever. I seemed to have a connection with these crystals, but not to own one. I was told a crystal was yours if it jumped out at you, because it was saying, 'I belong to you.' So I walked around the many trays of crystals and scanned for my crystal with my hand, as I was shown to do. But none jumped out at me. I never knew that was the way you picked a crystal, so with no crystal, I left the shop, feeling lighter and more serene from being in there.

My next stop-over was the capital city of Langford. I had a day there, and the next day I was off to Dolphin Point. On arrival in the town, I fell in love with it. So far, of all the places I had visited, this was paradise for me.

I found Peggy's house easily enough. She was in raptures to see me, and I met her adorable kids: Shelly, who was about fourteen, and Jerod, who was seven. I instantly loved Jerod. He looked very similar to my own Jerod at that age. Peggy was a short, red-faced, fair-haired, jolly lady with a happy disposition. She'd married a guy about ten years younger than herself, and they'd decided to come up here to live to be closer to his parents.

That day, we chatted and laughed and went for a walk around the incredible seafront area of Dolphin Point. Dolphin Point was an idyllic tropical paradise, with beautiful beaches and great surf, and a calmness in the air that was different to my own hometown, even though it too was a coastal town. Here, time wasn't of any urgency, and after being there for a couple of days, I didn't want to leave it and go back to Dawson Hill. The people here were warm-hearted and kind. I got to meet Peggy's husband's parents, and they were really lovely people who were so accepting of Peggy, even though she was much older than Monte, her husband. The parents loved Jerod a lot you could tell, and they accepted Shelly, who was from a different father, as their own. Peggy told me her first marriage was a mistake and that she'd married too young.

The more I stayed there, the less urgency I had to do things; everyone was so laidback. However, Peggy had to go to work, so her children and I went to many tourist places: the zoo, and to a museum. While we were out sightseeing and driving around, I came across a wonderful town called Paradise Cove, and that had to be the best place, on the whole, of the coastal towns I visited. I loved Dolphin Point; however, Paradise Cove topped it. It was a tropical paradise. As I travelled around this area, I could fully understand why Peggy wanted to live up this way.

It was a lovely holiday. I loved being with Peggy and her children; we all got on so well. At night-time, while lying in my bed, I contemplated my trip so far. I really felt I'd done the right thing by doing this trip, and how I loved to travel and be away from my own area.

Unfortunately, I didn't know what was waiting for me back home, and how my life on my own would be played out. Peggy and Monte had some disagreements, and it made me realise I didn't like conflict. After I witnessed their conflict, I was happy to move on. On the day I left, it was a sad goodbye. Peggy had asked me to come back and stay with them again. I told her I'd love to. Peggy seemed more natural and not so pretentious as she had been. I think she realised I saw what was really going on in their home. She'd showed how she really felt. I could see we all had our own stresses in our marriages, regardless of our happy exteriors and how we portrayed our lives on the outer side. I felt she had been putting on a happy face and showed me that.

On the way back, I stopped at Mitchell Point for a day and went swimming in the beautiful bay there, and then travelled down the coast, staying here and there overnight. I had plenty of time to call in and see Lucy and her family, so I called her to say I'd stop in again. She was pleased, and the next day I headed for Port Foxdale. There, we did some more sightseeing and went out to dinner as a treat from Randall and their daughter, Leigh. I should have been treating them, but he wouldn't hear of it.

Finally, it was time to face my life in Dawson Hill. On the journey back, I started to feel some sexual urges within myself. I'd never been a sexually aroused person, even with Javier. We'd had sex every day, and I was only freed from sex when I had a period. I was never turned on by him or desired sex or instigated sex. Maybe it was because I was so used to having sex every night with Javier. The sexual feeling got stronger, and I didn't want to go home like this and have to face these issues. Maybe I'd have to call him over.

So I played with my breasts as I travelled to relieve the feeling, and I had to touch myself, which I'd never done before. It wasn't nice to do that. I didn't like the idea of touching my private parts. But the urgency grew, and it was so painful to release it. I couldn't release it – I'd only ever had one orgasm in my life, when Bonnie-Claire was born; before that, I'd never felt in that area of my body. Why was this area of my body awakening now? Why now, when I was free from Javier? I talked myself out of this mayhem and soon stopped those feelings and felt my freedom again.

Chapter 32

Back In My House

For the first three months, I was in heaven at home. I stayed at home and never went out. I just cleaned the house and enjoyed my own company. I was pottering, and it was just great; I loved it. I was so happy, and I didn't want to go out or be connected to people – my contentment was with myself. Also, I started to visit my parents more often. Mum and I were becoming closer. I really felt good around her, because I was free from Javier. I asked Mum if she would support me in my life, if I ever needed her support. She immediately said she felt she always supported me. But I knew she hadn't in the past.

However, she agreed on that day to always be supportive of me if I ever needed it. I would regularly go and see my parents. On one visit, I found out some interesting news about Javier. He'd met a girl called Leigh on Friday, 24th October, the day after I'd left him. It didn't worry me, and I realised that he had to have company and couldn't live alone for too long. But I felt it was a bit quick. I left, and the next day he had another woman in his bed. I heard he'd met her at the

Diamond Club in Morton Dale. Nonetheless, it didn't worry me, and actually, I was pleased for him.

Leigh ended up being his lover for about eighteen months. I thought, Someone did want him after all. I used to wish for someone to take him away from me, but they never did. The more I pondered on it, the more I wondered if he'd known Leigh when we were together, because it was so quick; he met her, and she was sleeping with him that night. Maybe he knew her from the days he and Len went out to the football.

I do know how love can grab you so unexpectedly. That had happened to me with Simon, and that proved it could happen. Fortunately, with Simon, I knew deep down it was only an opening for me to leave Javier, and when he left work it took me a while to get him out of my system. However, he was now gone out of my being, and I felt he'd completed what he needed to complete with me. Somehow, I could see how life worked with the people who came into my life. They did what they had to do and then they left. I was free from Javier and from Simon and happy by myself; their jobs were over. I easily let Javier and Simon go mentally and lost all attachment to both.

Coming home also brought another family member to my doorstep: our pet dog, Candy. Javier had asked Jerod to ask me to take over looking after her. I didn't want to do this – I didn't want to take on any responsibilities after being so responsible all my life, and now he was doing this to me. Because Candy was so old, she needed lots of care, which meant vet care. I was just scraping through paying my house loan and living, and now this. But she was okay. I settled with her and did the best I could for her. She had developed a bad rash on her skin during our marriage breakdown, when I wasn't paying attention to her, and she also had some lumps on her body. But she was still lively. I bought creams for her rash and bathed her in special shampoo recommended by a vet. When Candy came to stay, so did a small kitten from nowhere, and they seemed to form a strong friendship.

So I was again being responsible. I called the kitten Kitty, and I was sure Candy and Kitty were communicating with each other. Even though Candy was old, she was still her mischievous self and would torment the cat. They'd often walk around the small yard together, which was mainly filled by the swimming pool, and I caught Candy actually pushing the cat into the pool and then pretending she didn't do anything at all.

Well, when I saw that I just laughed, and the cat struggled out of the pool. It was so funny to see that cat trying to scramble out of the pool and the dog acting as if she didn't know what had happened. They reminded me of my boys: Julian, the tormentor, and Jerod, the one who copped the torments.

To be continued

About The Author

I was born in the Hunter Valley in New South Wales, Australia, and am one of three siblings.

I've had quite an interesting life, venturing outside of my country, where I found the inspiration to write books.

My greatest love is writing.

My favourite pastimes include reading, painting, travelling and meeting people, and capturing these moments through photography.

My other passion is helping people to uncover childhood issues.

Through my own experiences and understanding the deeper aspects of my behaviour, stemming from my childhood experiences, through sexual abuse, patterns learned, behaviours adopted, I can now help other people uncover their core issues that are causing them pain in their adult life.

My website contains my Bio, links to purchase my books and reviews:
Website: www.christineucowinwriter.com
Email address: christine@christineucowinwriter.com
Amazon Central Authors Page:
www.amazon.com/author/christineucowinwriter